DYNAMIC ASSESSMENT IN COUPLE THERAPY

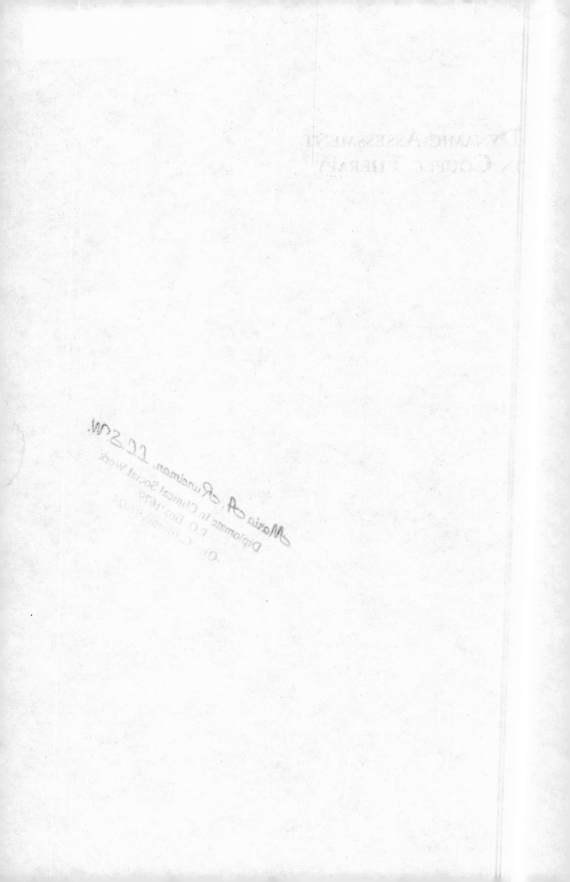

Dynamic Assessment in Couple Therapy

William J. Hiebert
Joseph P. Gillespie
Robert F. Stahmann

LEXINGTON BOOKS
An Imprint of Macmillan, Inc.
New York

Maxwell Macmillan Canada
Toronto

Maxwell Macmillan International
New York   Oxford   Singapore   Sydney

Library of Congress Cataloging-in-Publication Data

Hiebert, William J.
    Dynamic assessment in couple therapy / William J. Hiebert, Joseph
P. Gillespie, and Robert F. Stahmann.
        p.   cm.
    Includes index.
    ISBN 0-669-24863-0
    1. Family assessment.   2. Marital psychotherapy.   3. Interviewing
in psychiatry.   I. Gillespie, Joseph P.   II. Stahmann, Robert F.
III. Title.
RC488.53.H54   1993
616.89′156—dc20   93-11168
                                                             CIP

Lexington Books
An Imprint of Macmillan, Inc.
866 Third Avenue, New York, N.Y. 10022

Maxwell Macmillan Canada, Inc.
1200 Eglinton Avenue East
Suite 200
Don Mills, Ontario M3C 3N1

Macmillan, Inc. is part of the Maxwell Communication Group of Companies.

Printed in the United States of America

printing number
1 2 3 4 5 6 7 8 9 10

Contents

Contents

Preface

"Beyond this place, there be dragons." Cartographers wrote this phrase on the maps of five hundred years ago to indicate where their knowledge of the world ended. Among ancient mariners and explorers, the unmapped areas of the world conjured up fears of the unknown and, consequently, often inhibited people from venturing too far from familiar lands. If you chose to sail into uncharted waters, then you had to be prepared to accept the risks.

In an analogous way, couples seeking therapy might be struggling with both realistic fears and irrational perceptions as they attempt to chart a course of exploration into the unknown regions of their relationship. Unfortunately, once they are under sail, many couples discover that they in fact had loaded a cargo of dragons before they left port. As therapists, our task might be to examine the relationship maps they insist on using to try to get to where it is they think they want to go, and to help uncover and slay the real or imagined dragons they have triangulated into their relational journey.

We have found that the initial assessment and understanding of the dynamics of the couple are crucial for effective therapy, regardless of the theoretical approach that one takes.

In creating the Structured Initial Interview (SII), our hope is that the therapist will be able to help the couple clarify and confront their "dragons" and move beyond these initial complaints and fears. The outcome of careful assessment for the therapist and the couple will be a better understanding of individual and couple strengths and weaknesses, a clarification of therapy goals and expectations, and more appropriate treatment planning.

An ancient proverb states that "the longest journey begins with a single step." Our experience as therapists over the past twenty-five years coincides with the consistent data showing that increasing numbers of couples (married or unmarried, straight or gay) are seeking treatment before they take one more step in a wrong direction. Parallel to an increasing demand for therapy, there has been a marked increase in the need for helpful methods of assessment and treatment. Our goal in creating the methodology for using the SII is to present a helpful structure for the assessment of couples in the initial stages of treatment so that effective treatment planning and therapy outcomes can be achieved. The focus of *Dynamic Assessment in Couple Therapy* is the relationship of couples, although the ideas presented can easily be adopted to working with families.

Current debates about the future of marriage, the family, or committed couple relationships are often based on flawed misconceptions about the psychological function of human relationships. Even though recently released statistics from the Census Bureau seem indicate that Americans are marrying and remarrying less in the 1990s, it is clear that Americans will continue to seek relationships to satisfy the basic psychological, physical, and spiritual need for intimacy. Most people believe that this need for intimacy can be best fulfilled in some form of couple relationship. Traditional cultural and religious perceptions of what constitutes a "real" couple or family configuration have run head-on into hard statistical data indicating that fewer American couples and families meet these romanticized norms. Part of our clinical agenda in devising the SII has been to help couples understand the relational shifts that have taken place in their personal history and to seek ways to address dysfunctional dynamics without being judgmental.

Though it might seem axiomatic that most unhealthy relationships remain unhealthy in proportion to the inability of the partners to talk about real problems, we have found that just getting couples to talk about the real problems does not necessarily create any impetus for lasting change. The SII is envisioned as an invitation for the couple to see their relationship history unfolding within the context of identifying persisting patterns, themes, and pockets of resistance. We have approached the use of the SII from a systems perspective and are well aware of the dynamics of homeostasis. Helping the couple to identify what above all else they do not want changed by the process of the assessment can be the first real step in the right direction; disclosing their ownership of a vested interest in preserving a particular dragon often proves to be the necessary catalyst to jog their imagination into considering a possible change. Helping a couple to explore the stuckness of their relationship is really an opportunity for both partners to acknowledge the part they play in creating and maintaining their "pet dragons" in the relationship.

The SII is an imaginative exercise that can be shared by the clients and therapist alike. Creative ideas for change do not derive from simply recognizing personal experiences alone. Rather, an acknowledgement of the interactions of the assessment process allows therapist and clients a way to accept ownership of the couple's history, destructive patterns of persistent interaction, and rigid personal metaphors. The creative goal of the SII is to allow insights to emerge from the unfolding time line of the couple's history through the use of appropriate questions. The fashioning of therapeutic metaphors can and often does enable the couple to move toward a paradigmatic shift from destructive to constructive behavior.

Quite simply, the SII attempts to make sense out of what a couple is attempting to live through. This process can be experienced as both a curse and blessing. The SII is not about romanticizing a pathological relationship history, nor is it an attempt to turn a fairly happy couple history into a microscopic study of hidden flaws. There is no need to assume that the SII is a brand new form of enlightenment or the only assessment technique for ailing relationships. At best, and not in the least, the SII can teach couples to be less fearful in the exploration of their troubled relationship maps, to begin to challenge their pet dragons, and to risk taking a first step away from their repetitive, destructive patterns.

As authors we are indebted to our clients, who have patiently helped us to be aware of our own pet methodological dragons as we searched out their personal histories. Also, we are most appreciative of our students, supervisees, and colleagues, and our editor, Margaret Zusky, who have graciously allowed us to believe that we have somehow been able to draw better maps, devise reasonably fail-safe travel plans, and even build a better clinical "mousetrap" capable of capturing and slaying dragons.

DYNAMIC ASSESSMENT IN COUPLE THERAPY

1

Introduction and Overview

The map is not the territory any more than a photograph is a person. Both a map and a photograph, however, can offer the observer an orientation to finding the right place and meeting the right person. Though both the map and the photograph constitute frozen moments of time, place, and person, they can serve as living and dynamic metaphors for any therapist who wishes to practice the art of couple therapy. It is critical that such therapists have accurate ways of picturing who and what it is that they are working with and mapping where it is that clients have been, are, and want to go. Like expert cartographers and photographers, the couple therapist can help to depict scenarios and patterns in a relationship that have been a source of disorientation and poor focusing.

Couple therapy, from our perspective, is the systemic application of techniques or interventions intended to change the dysfunctional patterns and unfocused interactions found in the relationships of couples. The therapist (whether marriage and family therapist, psychologist, social worker, pastoral counselor, psychiatrist, or licensed counselor) can best help a couple (whether married or cohabitating, or straight, lesbian, or gay) by serving as an active consultant

1

to the relationship, not to one partner or the other. Thus, the focus of modification or change in the relationship is the relationship itself. Usually, and preferably, both partners are encouraged to be actively involved in the therapy sessions. In our model of therapy, the relationship or system is the primary subject of attention, and both partners become active participants in helping to chart the data and appropriate angles for therapeutic interventions and behavioral change.

As professionals working with and treating relationships, we have been and are closely identified with systems theory. Realizing that the simplest definition of a system is a series of parts interacting to achieve some goal(s), we attempt to focus on the dynamic relationship of these interacting parts as a way of understanding and modifying the dysfunctional interchanges of the system. Special attention must be paid to the normal resistance of any system to outside change; once a system (or relationship) gets set in motion, it is difficult to interrupt patterns of interaction, even if such change is desired.

The roles, rules, and rituals of any system demand that we pay attention to set patterns, lived history, and experiences of change attempts that somehow brought on the same old dysfunctional dynamic. We are aware that therapy with stuck systems is difficult and, in some cases, seemingly impossible.

From our systems perspective, we are interested in changing destructive patterns of interaction, not in destroying the system. To invite change, however, is to invite resistance and pain. Our hope and experience has been that invitations to healthy change often involve naming some very painful historical dynamics, claiming the resulting dysfunctional patterns of interaction, and taming the tendencies to change back to the dysfunctional patterns. Through the use of an assessment technique that we have designed, we have discovered some rather helpful ways of exploring such invitations.

Looking Ahead Through the Rearview Mirror

The Structured Initial Interview (SII), an assessment technique we developed, has been taught and used extensively in academic and clinical settings. The SII seems to have an immediate appeal to most students and clinicians because of its simplicity in handling and sorting out the complexity of couple histories, relationship patterns, and the subtle and repetitive resistive dynamics found in dysfunctional systems.

The SII engages students and clinicians alike because the methodology can quite literally draw the therapist, as well as the clients, into the graphic meandering of issues in any relationship. As the history of the relationship unfolds, so, too, do the interactional patterns that have been held in place by the unique roles, rules, and rituals of the system. The level of awareness and acceptance of dysfunctional patterns by the couple can then become the therapeutic ground upon which negotiations for remapping the direction of the relationship might take place.

It has been our clinical observation that couples who learn to address the dysfunctional dynamics of their relationship through a willingness to examine its historical goals can speak more candidly and less anxiously about its future. The SII provides an invitation to initiate this historical search and a process by which both the couple and the therapist can discover where dysfunctional dynamics and recurring patterns get in the way of desired change. Even for couples who are in the process of divorce or are separated, we have found that the use of the SII is experienced as less threatening than other forms of history taking and assessment. The level of resistance tends to lessen when it becomes clear that the SII does not attempt to make one of the participants an object of blame or scapegoating. Rather, the SII as an information-gathering technique focuses on the relationship of the couple and the interaction of these two individuals in this unique system.

As future chapters will demonstrate, the SII is similar to

other kinds of information-gathering techniques and can quite clearly be viewed as a way of inviting a therapeutic process to take place without labeling it as therapy. Our general experience has been that the SII can bind a couple's high anxiety levels, structure rather complex information, help to surface dysfunctional interaction patterns, and offer appropriate clues about what needs attention if change is to occur. Whether a couple wants to make use of the insights then becomes the basis either for contracting for continued therapy or for termination of the sessions. For some couples, the process of completing the SII seems to provide enough awareness to motivate them to initiate appropriate changes in their relationship without a continued professional context for assistance.

Treatment Considerations

For a therapist to work with a problematic relationship, a number of practical treatment considerations must be addressed. A specific discussion of critical steps to be taken with the implementation of the SII will be introduced in the following chapters. The following generic issues, however, influence both treatment form and the therapeutic effectiveness of treating relationships.

Client and Therapist Expectations

Undoubtedly, clients have some expectations about the therapy process and the desired outcomes. This is why one or both made contact initially and decided to keep the appointment. The therapist soon learns, however, that client expectations and motivations vary greatly. Thus, one case may involve two highly motivated partners who expect to work on their own problems and those of the relationship. Another couple may present themselves for therapy with one partner saying that the problem is with the other person, and that he or she is here to help the therapist "straighten out" the partner's problem. In such cases, it is obvious that the therapist will need to deal with expectations of the blaming partner as well as with those of the "identified patient." For the therapist to understand client expectations is crucial for effective therapy; clients often can and do have incorrect ideas about therapy and what constitutes healthy change.

The therapist also has expectations in regard to therapy that the couple must understand. Basic therapist expectations include the point of view that the problem lies in what is happening (or not happening) between the partners, not only with one individual, and that the therapist has no conscious alliances with either partner. In identifying the relationship as the problem or "patient," it becomes the focus of intervention and change. It bears repeating that when we introduce the SII as the process for examining the presenting problem(s), it is very important that the couple be helped to defuse their need to blame one another as the problem. Only then can we focus on the history of the couple's relationship. In many ways, the SII can help to spread the pain and the blame around and lessen the danger of unhealthy collusion or polarization.

Structure and Control

As therapy is initiated, a critical issue facing all therapists and clients is who is in charge of the therapy. Simply because the clients have actively sought out therapy, it cannot be assumed that they have, in fact, relinquished control to the therapist. The therapist must negotiate control rather quickly during the first session. As the therapist clarifies the expectations of the couple, the role of the therapist, and the techniques to be used, it is highly encouraged that an active participation on the part of both therapist and clients is understood and expected. Other expectations and issues regarding the use of SII (or of the genogram, various forms of psychological testing, therapeutic homework, and so on) need to be explained in a candid and understandable manner.

The Therapeutic Triangle

Even though the focus of the intervention and therapy is the relationship, with the inclusion of the therapist, something changes with the client system. The client dyad now becomes a triad, and the interaction of the parts of the clients' system is juxtaposed with a new tension. The human triangle in family theory is commonly thought to be the basic unit of human interaction, and the most primitive dynamic of the human triangle is that two persons are involved in the main current of interaction and one person ends up as an observer. To be sure, the observer has a part to play in the emotional triangle and can exert power; when crises occur in very troubled relationships, the dyad often polarizes rather predictably, and one or both partners go in search of a third party to draw into the tension. Whether or not an observer (in this case, the therapist) can effectively modify the dysfunctional dynamics of the system remains to be seen. How the role of this new part might fit into the dysfunctional system becomes the creative and challenging task of the therapist.

Generally speaking, the therapeutic triangle yields at least three interactional combinations for the systems-oriented therapist. In the *mediation* configuration, one person (usually the therapist) serves to balance and arbitrate the relationship between the other two persons. In an *alliance* configuration, two persons are attempting to help the third. Such could be the situation when the therapist and one spouse agree on the idea of an "identified patient" as the real problem. In the *collusion* configuration, there is the dynamic of two persons lining up against the third. Although it is usually not the conscious intent of the couple to gang up on the therapist when they enter therapy, a skillful therapist can identify this dynamic and use it as a powerful basis for change on behalf of the couple. "Stumping the therapist" may not be the name clients might admit to, but the dynamic can easily come into play when the therapist comes too close to really changing the system. Unfortunately, for some dysfunctional systems, the pain seems to be preferred.

Contracting

A final important area of concern for the therapist is called *contracting*—the process of setting limits and building reasonable expectations with clients. Contracting is a way of letting clients know that the therapist expects a modification in the outcome of the dysfunctional relationship. If the therapist cannot get some agreement regarding the suggested outcome, then it is doubtful that an ethical contract can be agreed upon. Assuming that an agreed level of healthy exploration can take place, the therapist can introduce the structure to be used in therapy. Lengths of sessions and frequency will depend on a number of factors, including how long the couple has been in the relationship, what expectations they are in agreement on, and fee schedules, as well as the time commitments of therapist. (When we explore the actual use of the SII, the sense of how much time will be necessary, including session frequency, will be better understood.) Generally speaking, we have found that weekly sessions work best for the beginning and middle course of therapy. The interval between sessions can increase as termination of therapy approaches.

"Plus Ça Change, Plus C'est la Même Chose"

The old French proverb of "the more things change, the more they remain the same" leads us into the difficult dilemmas of working with patterns. We are confident that when a therapist can find an accurate methodology for helping couples frame their history, then the emergence of a particular pattern can be recognized. It is in the emergence and recognition of this pattern that conscious intervention techniques can be suggested. Creating the possibility of concrete change is very important, but it must be based on clients' willingness to own the dysfunctional pattern and to work toward the formation of therapeutic change. In many ways, the therapist is there to encourage the couple as they challenge the pattern that has created the dysfunctional relationship. The formulation and the implementation of change are filled with challenges and resistance. With the use of appropriate structural treatment considerations and of the SII, however, we have found the level of resistance to be diminished.

The following chapters invite you to understand the administrative issues in couple assessment, to utilize the SII as an assessment technique for exploring a couple's history and style of interaction, and to examine some commonly recurring couple patterns. We will be using a complete case history to understand the subtle process of the SII, as well as offering guidelines about how to ask appropriate questions regarding themes and patterns. We are well aware, of course, that techniques are used only until the real therapist can provide his or her own input. Until the naturalness of the therapeutic relationship offers its own healing insights, however, we invite you to explore some ways to help map and photograph a couple's relationship.

2
Administration Issues in Couple Assessment

One of the most important lessons for a therapist to learn is the art of structuring the initial interview, which actually takes several sessions. We call this an art simply because it requires a great deal of experience as well as experimentation, feeling, and technique. It also, however, requires an element of scientific methodology to ensure some consistency and reasonable predictability.

Couples coming for therapy very often do so with very vague complaints about what is wrong with their relationship. In using the SII evaluation, the therapist will be able to help the couple clarify (as well as take ownership of) these difficulties. The SII will help them to experience the history of their relationship in a unique way.

In effect, the couple is asked to make a specific contract to look at their courtship and relationship history in a way that begins with information to which they both have access. If the couple agrees to such a contract, therapy begins by doing just that. By presenting the couple with an invitation to spend one to four sessions looking at their own history, the therapist not only reduces anxiety but also postpones any need to make a decision about the dysfunction and/or health of the relationship.

The rationale for the SII can be summarized in the following points:

1. It provides a sense of direction for the therapist and the couple in therapy.
2. It helps the therapist understand that he or she needs the couple's participation to gather information about them.
3. It helps to unravel the tapestry of the courtship and relationship histories in a safe setting.
4. It changes the agenda from crisis counseling to an evaluation.
5. It creates a sense of movement and participation (healthy collusion) on the part of the couple.
6. It gives the couple a model for asking questions.

Healthy Collusion

With much skill and some luck, the cooperative adventure between the therapist and the clients bring with it a movement away from scapegoating and identified-patient syndromes. Looking at the clients' interaction from a historical point of view moves the focus of attention from the individuals to their joint relational experience. At this point, there is a shift from individual responsibility or faultfinding to an exploration of mutual decisions, dreams and goals, and successes and failures.

In this context, the therapist can avoid the self-congratulatory impulses of being the all-knowing expert on the relationship. The point to be emphasized and understood is that there are two people involved in this system, and that they are both necessary to maintain the health or sickness of the relationship.

Dismantling the Totems and Taboos

The anxiety level of all of us increases when our secrets are talked about. When we are able to take ownership of our secrets, however, then we are able to take responsibility for either talking about them or continuing to try to hide them. The therapist, through the SII, is able to take the couple through their own shared secrets and help them to talk in a way that makes the secrets less threatening.

More often that not, much information comes out in the initial interview that was never talked about by the couple previously. Sometimes this can be a very frightening experience for the couple, inasmuch as they claim that they never knew a given fact about the other person or that they really felt a given way about some event. The areas of sex, in-laws, and unfulfilled dreams often are experienced as sources of buried anger and real frustration. When the therapist can, through his or her questions, create at atmosphere in which the old "totems and taboos" are talked about and viewed objectively, then the couple can begin to release themselves from the clutches of these binding memories.

Healthy Questions

We have discovered that asking the right questions can give the couple and the therapist important answers. Though this may sound rather simplistic, it is our experience that when we are able to ask questions that make sense, the couple is able to respond in a joint effort with answers that make sense. The "right questions" help us to do the following:

- Ask questions that are answerable because they are related to factual experiences ("In what year were you married?" "How did you meet?" "What did you like about each other?")
- Create a model for dealing with taboo or touchy issues by bringing them up in a clinical setting ("Does your partner's obesity make it difficult for you to enjoy him?")

- Formulate hunches about who is in charge of the relationship ("How did you decide what to do on dates?" "How did you decide to handle your money?" "Who is in charge of your social life?")

- Understand key areas of resistance ("What caused you to drop out of therapy before coming here?")

- Create a tentative diagnosis of the interactional pattern operating with this couple ("Do either of you recognize a pattern of repetition here?")

The Time Factor

All therapists are bound by time and, as such, require techniques to help them quickly get to the root of the problems in therapy. Often, however, the major complaint of couples who drop out revolves around the "timeless" approach of the therapist. This open-ended approach borders on the unendurable for even the most dependent clients and, in many ways, bespeaks the need for therapists to understand that although time is a healing factor, awareness, confrontation, healing, and change can be promoted in a matter of a few structured interviews.

We have come to view the SII as a way of implementing therapy immediately without really having to call it therapy. We have discovered that using the SII helps couples to look at their history as well as the possibility of their future together.

Commitment and Contract

We have discovered that it is absolutely crucial to try to clarify, from the very beginning, the level of commitment the clients have to each other and to looking at their relationship. When we have a sense of bonding in the relationship, then we can begin to look for an agreement to do the SII. This in turn allows us to look at the material with a sense of objectivity, as well as to postpone making any decisions about remaining as a couple or separating.

We are well aware that it is often difficult to determine a couple's problem during the first session. The SII, therefore, can be postponed until the therapist has some sense of direction and/or feeling of commitment from the couple. It is the clients' decision about their relationship that is at stake. We do believe however, that we must have some sense of agreement and commitment if we are to proceed with the SII.

Contradictions

There are couples whose goals are so divergent, or whose conflict is so chronic, that any real change in their relationship seems unlikely. If the therapist senses chronic resistance to change in the first session, perhaps the SII should not be begun, nor therapy continued. We have discovered that there are at least four factors that contraindicate the use of the SII:

1. One party wants out of the relationship and makes that clear.
2. There is a real hesitancy on the part of one party to participate in the SII.
3. The couple requires a different form of treatment (for example, one is seriously psychotic and needs a psychiatric referral).
4. The immaturity of the couple or the chronicity of the conflict precludes any real climate for change and seriousness in therapy.

In these instances, we have found it helpful for both ourselves and the couple to confront them with our observations and/or unwillingness to keep them in therapy. We willingly refer such couples to other professionals for another opinion.

Technique and Style

Creating a model for an SII is not difficult. It has been our experience, however, that it is important not to rush to the end of the history in a desire to deal with the "real" dysfunctional issues. Each partner has a story to tell, and the therapist has much to learn. Unfortunately, conclusions can be drawn at the expense of confusing and discouraging clients. Getting at the "real" issues and identifying them too soon can scare clients away. By using a casual but attentive style, the therapist can set a pace that will allow him or her to act as a chronicler of the couple's relational history. Moving slowly and efficiently can help to paint a realistic picture of their lives together. In some ways, it is like asking a couple to sit for a portrait and, at the same time, to help in the painting of it.

Use of Visual Techniques

What might be of use to the therapist, at this point, is a white-board or newsprint. We have found that the external-ization of the history helps the couple to visualize their own time line and sense of historical development. In many instances, we have found that simply illustrating the key dates and movements in the relationship has helped the couple to relax and talk together about their experience; a sense of involvement heightens when there is disagreement upon key dates or events. The therapist, as well as the couple, can focus on the visual aid as a way of creating a shared experience in therapy. Often, too, the therapist gets a chance to observe how people relate to their history and can begin to sense the affect level of the couple when talking about it. In general, the use of the SII has helped us to create a sense of activity and involvement in the couple's history.

Use of the white-board has the advantage of ease in erasing. It requires the therapist, however, to keep notes on significant events and experiences. Newsprint has the advantage of potentially being saved for use in later sessions.

Sometimes couples are asked to take the chalk or pen in hand themselves and to sketch significant dates, events, or interactional diagrams on the board or paper. A sample chart is shown in Table 2–1.

More on the Contract

When the therapist has been assured that there are no contraindications for doing the SII, when all of the verbal and nonverbal signals appear to be "go," the therapist's next task is to propose an evaluation of the relationship. The evaluation process is the SII.

Length of the SII. Before going ahead, it is important to remark that the SII, in our conceptualization, can be anywhere

Table 2–1
A Sample SII of the Courtship Phase of a Couple's Evaluation

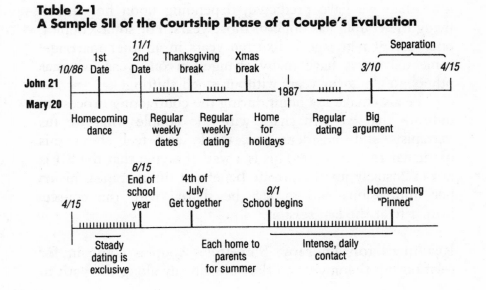

from one to four sessions, each one and a half hours in length. It is important, therefore, in making the contract with the couple to give them as estimation of the time it will take to accomplish the SII. We have found this rule of thumb helpful: if the couple has been married or has cohabited for less than five years, one or two sessions will be needed (including the first session); five to ten years, two or three sessions; and more than ten years, three or four sessions.

In regard to the contracting, we have found it advantageous to give the therapist some leeway, as shown above. At the same time we have found it helpful to indicate that we will not go beyond the predicted maximum number of sessions without doing so by the mutual agreement of all parties.

Rationale for Assessment. Some comment about time is also helpful in the contracting process. Some people are taken aback that the therapist would want to spend so much time evaluating the relationship. This can be handled easily by making use of the analogy that few people would go to a physician who prescribed medication without taking the time to figure out what the medicine was for. In addition, we have found it helpful to indicate that we might use more or less time than we have predicted, depending upon how much living the couple has done in those years. For some couples, one year of marriage is like ten years in another marriage; some marriages have many changes in one year, whereas others go along for years without much shifting.

We also make it a point during the contracting process to indicate that we will share with the couple what we (as therapists and outsiders) see, think, and feel about this particular relationship. This is a way of saying that the SII is not exclusively for the private benefit of the therapist: his or her impressions will in fact be shared with the couple, primarily at the last session.

Readiness for Therapy. Sometimes couples come in for relationship therapy when they are already along the path to a dissolution. The exploration of the relationship, therefore, provides us some clues as to where they are along the dissolution line and whether either partner has secretly made a decision about the relationship.

While the therapist is involved in conducting the SII, he or she has an opportunity to get some sense of whether the couple is ready for therapy. Are the partners interested in seeing how each can change and how each contributes to the system? Are they in therapy because they want the therapist to determine who is right and who is wrong in the relationship? Or do they want the therapist to baby-sit while one goes ahead and gets a divorce or leaves the relationship?

The use of the contract to evaluate the relationship allows the therapist the opportunity to end the therapy or refer the couple. Sometimes, in fact, couples are not ready for therapy or are not coming for productive reasons. To determine that a couple is not ready for therapy is helpful both for the couple and the therapist.

Therapeutic Boundary Issues

The SII is predicated on the idea that therapists have a tendency either to become too involved with or to remain too distant from the couple. Therapists who get too involved and become triangulated into the couple's relationship often do so because they jump immediately into exploring the dynamics and interaction of the couple. Therapists who remain too cool and distant, in contrast, often become nonpersons in the sessions by virtue of their nonparticipation style. The SII is a useful technique in trying to steer between these two extremes. It provides enough interaction for the couple to experience the therapist as a person and helps them gain perspective and outside information. At the same time, it provides an appropriate amount of distance to facilitate the therapist's determination of how and where to intervene in the system.

The last comment we make to couples before beginning the SII may come as a surprise to some. We indicate that the SII is neither therapy nor counseling; rather, it will be an opportunity for the therapist(s) to get to know what it is like to be in the relationship, and for the couple to determine whether they would like to work with the therapist(s). When we complete the SII and do the wrap-up, we may then propose a new contract. This contract could be for therapy, for focused work on a specific aspect of their relationship (such as their sexual relationship, or communication), or for termination.

We present the SII as not being therapy because we think it important that clients not try to change before they have really decided they want to change. A seasoned therapist will respect the timing of clients in this matter.

Conclusion

What the therapist looks for when conducting the SII will depend upon his or her perspective on relationships. The areas we outline in this book tell a great deal about how we perceive couple interaction and what our own perspective is. Although the areas of focus we list indicate how we have organized the material, however, the SII is not to be viewed as ours. It is a technique that can be shaped by any therapist, adding or subtracting areas of focus depending upon his or her own preferences.

It is important to remember that we view the SII as multiphasic. On the one hand, it allows the couple to disclose their relationship to the therapist in terms and in ways that they understand. On the other hand, it allows the therapist to think on another level, looking at the material with his or her own perspective.

In the next chapter, we will explain some interaction patterns that we have observed in clients' relationships. Though it is not our intention to categorize or pigeonhole relationships, we have found it helpful for therapists to have "relationship maps" as they begin an orientation process with couples. These maps can help the therapist to understand why there might be resistance on the part of the couple to changing directions in terms of their dysfunctional dynamics, and what couples might do to prevent the therapist from effecting therapeutic interventions.

3

Background Maps for the Therapist: Common Couple Interaction Patterns

Behind our definition of couple therapy is an assumption about relationships. We assume that couple relationships have some purpose, that they make sense. We assume that people marry or cohabit to meet needs. When the needs of both partners are met, the relationship can be described as functional. When they are not met or are out of balance, the relationship becomes problematic.

Couple therapy with a relationship focus has different goals than couple therapy with an individual perspective. Rather than being a process of resolving individual conflicts, couple therapy with a relationship focus is a process of awareness. Couple therapy, then, becomes an invitation to experience and become aware of what the partners do to each other, a searching for links to their mutual involvement, responsibilities, and complementary patterns.

This chapter assumes that relationship work is not so much a search for *why* but for *what* partners do for and/or to each other. If couples can be helped to see their functional and dysfunctional patterns of interaction, they can be helped immeasurably toward preserving or renegotiating the health of the relationship. If couples not only see what they do to each other but choose to change it, they will be helped in making choices that can promote healthy change.

Development of Patterns

Knowledge of common couple interaction patterns has several benefits for therapists. First, the patterns enable therapists to "see" systems more expeditiously. Second, by being able to spot clues of a particular pattern during the SII, the therapist is able to pursue the evaluation process during the initial interviews with a greater sense of direction (that is, to shape the questions during the SII to identify a possible recurring pattern). Third, therapists whose insight has been sharpened to spot patterns have a greater sense of confidence in working with couples and a sense of direction in regard to treatment and treatment choices.

Before discussing the patterns, we would like to caution the reader about four issues. First, the patterns listed here are presented in highlight fashion. To use an analogy from art, we are sketching a basic outline on the canvas that will be filled in and painted by your actual clients. Our task is to highlight and emphasize the basic shape; in order to do that, we will at times make use of stereotypes. Second, the patterns are designed to be descriptive. Space will not be taken to raise conceptual issues regarding the nature of the human personality or the ideology and conceptual frameworks regarding various emotions and behaviors.

Third, the patterns have their value in flexibility. We caution the reader against seeing them as rigid categories, inflexible bins in which to dump relationships. Rather, they are to be viewed with the realization that some couple interactions will more closely resemble one style, whereas others will have bits and pieces from various styles, and still others will be found nowhere among the styles.

Fourth, the various patterns have little to do with gender. Although we will characterize each style with given behavior for the male and female, it is important to remember that in most of the styles the behavior can be reversed. Though in many of the patterns it will be more common to see the male behave in one way and the female in another, most practitioners will also see the reverse. Obviously, cultural conditioning has a great deal to do with the roles males and females play in these various patterns. For same-sex couples, many of these patterns are also applicable, even though gender difference is not present.

The Half-Marriage

Bella and Jack have been married for thirty-eight years; Jack is fifty-six, and Bella is fifty-four. They were married in July 1955 after dating for two years, a courtship that was rather stormy with frequent fights. When Bella discovered that she was pregnant, Jack asked to marry her. Their first child was born in November 1955, a second in December 1957, and a third child in July 1968. Both Jack and Bella have been employed since the early years of their marriage.

Jack's drinking has been problem for many years; he entered alcoholism treatment in 1961 and in 1974. In the course of their marriage, they have been separated five times (in 1958, 1962, 1969, 1978, and 1988). Usually, the separations lasted about three months. Bella has belonged to Al-Anon, Weight Watchers, and a variety of church organizations throughout the length of the marriage. Jack, who is an on-and-off member of Alcoholics Anonymous, has few friends and is a loner.

Jack and Bella are friendly with their neighbors (they have lived in the same neighborhood and home for 35 years), but they rarely entertain or go out together. Jack dislikes being told what to do and claims that he is henpecked. When he and Bella get to fighting, he generally retreats to the basement or the garage. Bella claims that Jack is a workaholic and spends a great deal of his time at work. Both of them recognize that their fighting "leads" to separations and drinking bouts, but somehow they always seem to work it out and get back together. They are not opposed to couple therapy, but each of them sees the other as not interested in changing very much. Jack's most current arrest for drunk driving has prompted therapy.

SII: Half-Marriage

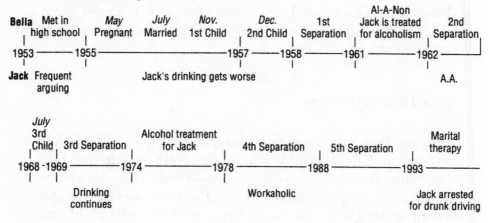

Description

The half marriage is perhaps the easiest of all patterns to see because it occurs commonly in couple counseling populations. In fact, bits and pieces of this particular style/pattern also can be found in other styles.

When a couple fitting this pattern enter the therapist's office for the initial session, their behaviors usually appear quite different and are easily identifiable. The male appears as a retiring, retreating, nonverbal person, whereas the female appears to be verbal and forward. The male retires from confrontation in the interaction, generally avoiding the direct expression of negativity and anger. His passive style is in contrast to his partner, who reports negativeness and anger in the marriage with greater ease. The partner's confrontational style of dealing with disappointments and pain can often be characterized as aggression.

Although the man's passive style and the woman's aggressive style appear in marked contrast on the outside, they are rather similar human beings on the inside. Both of these people can be described as having marked dependency needs. Both of them want very much to lean on the other person, both want to be taken care of, and both want the other to be strong. At the same time, however, both individuals experience their dependency with a great deal of pain. Each feels helpless and small in contrast to the partner or to other people. Both experience dependency with a great deal of distaste, and they despite that quality of their personality.

In an attempt to appear to be the strong partner that the other wants and to prevent the partner and other people from seeing his or her own sense of smallness and helplessness, each goes about building an elaborate protection of that vulnerable side. The female covers her dependency needs in two ways. First, she frequently behaves in a pseudoindependent style, perhaps involving herself in various community activities in an attempt to appear as though she does not need her partner, as though she can do things on her own. If one examined her community activities, however, one would see that although she attended, she was not really very connected or emotionally engaged with the other participants. Second, the female often covers her marked dependency needs with a veil of anger. By being angry, she protects herself from being seen as dependent or weak, and at the same time manages to convince herself and other people that her unhappiness is the fault of her weak partner. The male, by contrast, covers his dependency needs by a sense of reserve and a lack of emotional expressiveness —in short, by retreating into himself.

As the conflict in this relationship mounts, each person feels that he or she is not being taken care of and becomes suspicious that the other person is not as strong as he or she thought and is not doing the job of taking care of him or her. As the female becomes more aggressive in attempting both to get taken care of and to convince the male that he is not doing his job, he becomes more and more removed from the interaction, withdrawing more and more into himself.

Both of these individuals also have poor self-concepts;

their self-esteem is suffering. Each feels unattractive in some way, and their nonverbal behavior often reflects their low self-esteem.

This couple often experiences difficulty sexually. She, emanating anger in her aggressive style, frequently complains about the sexual relationship, with the result that he becomes less initiatory in the relationship and less interested in it. As the relationship cools sexually, the female becomes more angry about the partner's retreat. Typically, while she complains about his lack of assertiveness, his difficulty maintaining erection, or his difficulty with premature ejaculation, she also has difficulties, frequently being nonorgasmic. Thus, a sense of apathy overtakes the sexual aspect of the relationship. The male's behavior as described here can be observed, although he does not voice his complaints with as much flair. He is withdrawn, isolated, and lonely. (Remember, these patterns can appear with the genders in reversed behaviors.)

Predictable Pattern Clues

There are a number of behaviors that are typical of this particular relationship pattern and may help the therapist spot it more quickly. For one thing, such couples experience frequent ups and downs. Although their relationship often survives many years, it does so with many arguments and separations. At times this couple will separate, but the relationship will perpetuate itself after the divorce or breakup, occasionally with some improvement.

The behavior that we have described as typical of the female (although, as noted earlier, the positions could easily be reversed) can be spotted easily. She is the kind of person who will say, "How come you didn't wave to me when I was downtown yesterday?" or "Why don't you ever visit me?" In each case, the question is designed to put the receiver on the defensive. It makes the subtle assumption that the receiver is responsible for the other's health and happiness, and it also protects the sender from disclosing that he or she was hurt because the receiver did not wave, say hello, or come over to visit.

The Attaching-Detaching Marriage

Jim and Louise could easily be described as a nice and very attractive couple. Both Louise and Jim are well dressed, attracted to one another, and easy to talk with. Louise describes Jim as the kindest and nicest person she has ever met; Jim thinks that Louise is a fun person and a lovely companion and mother to their children. They describe their social life as very full, and they love to attend educational and cultural activities. Both Jim and Louise are teachers and have multiple social responsibilities. They have been married for twelve years and have two children—Billy, age ten, and Kate, age eight. They recently moved into a new home and are in the process of establishing themselves in the neighborhood. As a couple, they feel fortunate to have in-laws that they like and close ties with their families of origin.

Louise and Jim met while they were in college; she was a senior, and he was a junior. An "ideal couple," she was a cheerleader, and he played on the varsity football team. A storybook-romance aura seemed to surround them, and even when they experienced tension around differences in their personalities, college friends and family members always seemed to convince them that they were made for each other. Early on in their courtship (and continuing into their marriage) Louise noticed that Jim has a way of withdrawing emotionally, which she has often blamed on things she has said or done. Though Jim was appreciative of Louise's attention, he often felt that she was smothering him and wanted to control his behavior. Jim often found refuge in sports and in studies.

Many of the fights they have had revolved around his distancing behavior. In the early years of the marriage, Louise twice accused Jim of being involved with other women. Jim dismissed these accusations as silly and immature. He gets the feeling that when he does try to connect with Louise, she is not interested in him. In fact, the reason that they are in therapy now is as a result of Louise filing for a divorce, even though she claims she does not really want one. Jim suspects that she is involved with another man.

SII: Attaching-Demanding

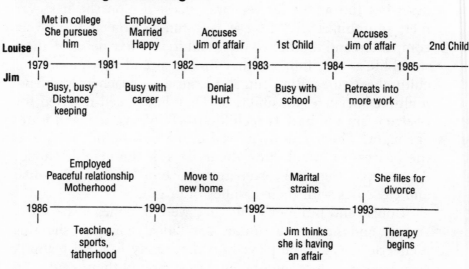

Description

This couple's initial appearance in the office is often met with surprise by the therapist. Both partners appear to function well in their relationship roles, in their respective careers, and in managing the financial aspects of the couple. In other words, on the surface, both seem to be successful people.

This particular couple experiences a struggle with intimacy. As the relationship begins to develop, the female begins trying to "heat up" the marriage, attempting to get closer to her partner and to get him to fulfill her various needs. She is looking for proof that he loves her, that he accepts her. As she accelerates her demands, attempting to get closer to her partner (attaching), he begins to back away (detaching). The closer she pushes, the farther away he moves.

As the therapist observes this couple, it is not difficult to see that the wife is determined to penetrate the husband's shell. In a very persistent manner, she struggles to win his love, to maneuver him into some statement proving that he does love her. The more she increases her pressure, the farther he goes into his protective shell. He can become very inexpressive, watching very carefully that he does not give his partner any clue to what he is really thinking and feeling on the inside. As the relationship engenders greater conflict, the female will frequently become very disillusioned, giving way to outbursts of anger. Yet the more she rages, the more he withdraws.

This relationship frequently has a kind of cycle about it. First, the wife will attempt to get closer to the husband, to do and say things that are designed to please him and win from him some statement of approval. She does this because she thinks she needs to earn his love. After this has gone on for a while, the second stage comes about, during which she decides that she should not have to win his affection, that it ought to just be there. When she finally decides that she should not need to win his love, she becomes angry and explodes. Following the explosion and a period of time, the cycle begins over again, with the wife going back to stage one. Though this couple on the outside appears to be very different, they are really both very sensitive people and easily hurt. (Again, remember that these patterns can appear with the gender behaviors reversed.)

Predictable Pattern Clues

There are several aspects of this relationship that provide excellent clues to its existence. When doing the SII, for example, this couple is often easy to spot. First, there is frequently a marked contrast in their behavior. During the early dating experiences, she often appeared as a very vivacious, fun, strong, and independent woman. He was attracted to this because she lent a sense of ease and comfortableness to their dating and frequently facilitated their social life. The male, on the other hand, appeared to be the strong, silent, and reliable type. She was attracted to this personality because she saw him as the kind of person who could take care of her and who would give her a sense of purpose and direction in life.

Another interesting dynamic of the courtship experience with this couple is that the one with the attaching style is often more active in attempting to cement the relationship. Sometimes this takes the shape of her becoming pregnant before marriage plans are firmed up, or initiating plans to live together.

During therapy, the interaction is often clear. Several metaphors come to mind. She appears to be an exotic dancer dancing around a great stone sphinx, convinced that somehow, if she can only dance creatively and exotically enough, the great stone sphinx might at least wink. Or she keeps attempting to light some kind of fire under him, hoping to melt the ice in which he seems to be encased. At points in the relationship she will attempt to jab a pin into him and pull it out to see if there is blood on the end, to see if he really is alive. To use another metaphor, each time she steals downstairs to turn the thermostat of the marriage higher, he sneaks in when she goes away and turns it back down to fifty degrees.

The Alienating Relationship

Stan and Beth have been living together for nine years; both have been previously married and divorced. Beth brought four children from her first marriage, and together Beth and Stan have had two children (Stan, Jr., age nine, and Judy, age five). They are currently living in a new housing development and are "up to their ears in debt;" Stan works as an independent supplier to motorcycle shops. Stan generally dresses in jeans, combat boots, and T-shirts (usually with the sleeves rolled up to hold a pack of cigarettes). He has a tendency to swagger when he walks, is in the habit of flexing his muscles as he sits, and seems proud of the tattoos acquired during his marine days. He is an odd study with an appearance of self-confidence and poise. Beth is a real contrast; she appears shrinking in style and physically limp when she sits in a chair. She seems to be tired and exhausted. "When she wants to get her act together, she can do just that," according to Stan. Beth claims that she is afraid of Stan, especially if he has been drinking or when he explodes with anger.

A recent domestic fight prompted police intervention. According to Beth, she had not cleaned the house to Stan's satisfaction, and he beat her up. Domestic violence was reported in 1984, 1985, 1987, and in 1989. After the 1989 dispute, Beth and the children moved into a "safe house" until Stan agreed to get help. They were in family therapy for one year. One of Stan's complaints has to do with a lack of sexual satisfaction in their marriage. Beth claims she is too exhausted from housework and taking care of children to be interested in sex.

SII: Alienating Relationship

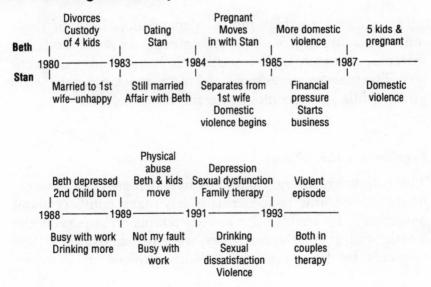

Description

When this couple first comes into the therapist's office, their behavior will be very clear. He will behave in an aggressive fashion, being openly angry and perhaps hostile. She, in contrast, will be rather passive. As the interaction develops, he will become alienating in his anger, attacking his partner in a belittling manner. The female will appear to be exceedingly submissive and dependent. She will take all of his barbs, accepting them as though she thinks she deserves them. The more he attacks, the more she gives in; the more she gives in, the more he attacks.

Despite their external differences, this couple (like those described previously) has similarities on the inside. Both individuals are exceedingly dependent, both wanting to be taken care of, and both wanting very much to have the other be a good "parent." But although they are both very dependent, they deal with their dependency rather differently. He deals with his by attempting to hide it, by behaving as the supermasculine male. She more openly acknowledges her dependency, acting as if she knows she does not have much of a partner, but he is the best she deserves and she will make the best of it.

In addition to their mutual dependency, both of these individuals suffer from low self-esteem. As such, both are insecure, although their insecurity is handled in a different way. The male becomes more and more attacking as the years go on, while she becomes more and more helpless.

Predictable Pattern Clues

This couple has several clues to its style that are generally easy to spot. First, this couple usually has many conflicts about housework. Invariably, the male attempts to supervise the female and regularly interferes with her housework. She responds by being exceedingly disorganized in domestic affairs. She appears to be a totally incapable, very disheveled, and disorganized person. A second clue to this particular couple is their sexual behavior. Frequently she complains about his roughness in their sexual relationship, whereas he complains that she is nonorgasmic.

In terms of their behavior, the style will be repeated over and over again. He will blame her for difficulties in the relationship and for her ineptness. The more he blames, the more she seems to accept the blame. After this goes on for a period of time, however, the wife will become frustrated with his needling and react by exploding. It is at this point, where she has reached her limits, that the couple will usually come for help.

The Child Relationship

Bobbie (age 28) and Norman (age 31) have had a very action-oriented marriage from the start in 1986. Both had been previously married and were involved in multiple affairs while married; in fact, it was during an affair with each other in 1985 that Bobbie's first husband shot Norman. Though he escaped serious injury, the shooting prompted them to settle down and get married. The court had awarded custody of Bobbie's two children to her parents and Norman's three children to his ex-wife. Right from the beginning of their marriage, both were suspicious of each other's activities and often complained to the other partner's parents about getting their son or daughter in line. Bobbie has separated from Norman on many occasions (1987, 1988, 1990, and 1993) and usually ended up living with her parents. Many times Norman would leave Bobbie and stay with his parents or his ex-wife. Bobbie claims that he is involved with his ex-wife.

The most recent fight prompted neighbors to call the police. Apparently Norman had purchased new racing tires for his car and discovered that his check had bounced. Bobbie had purchased a new television and VCR and depleted most of their savings and checking accounts. After cutting up three of Bobbie's dresses, Norman left in a rage, careening down the street in the car and almost hitting some neighbors' children. When Bobbie found the dresses, she took all of Norman's suits and threw them into the driveway. When he came back later that night and ran over the suits, he went wild. He broke the door down and was threatening to kill Bobbie. It was then that the neighbors called the police.

In a kind of childlike way, both Norman and Bobbie felt hurt and taken advantage of by each other. Both her and his parents accompanied them to the therapist's office.

SII: Child Relationship

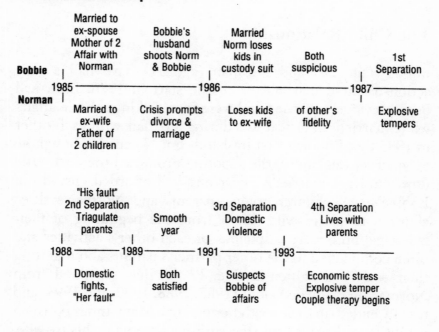

Description

The child relationship contains two individuals who are essentially children. Each wants the other to be the adult; at the same time, both behave in childish ways, want childish gratification, and are prone to temper tantrums or violence when they do not get their way.

Both of the individuals in this child marriage usually experience themselves as little and empty. They rarely see themselves as having anything to offer the other person. Both usually experience deep loneliness and desire affection from the other person, but neither is very capable of giving affection. This can also be seen in the area of health: each wants to be taken care of when sick, but each experiences the other's illness as an inconvenience and a pain.

Both of these individuals are still very tied to their family of origin. As such, the parents frequently interfere in the relationship, and a general state of bedlam exists as this couple is buffeted from side to side in a multigenerational struggle.

Predictable Pattern Clues

One important clue to this particular interaction is the way in which the partners structure the relationship. Frequently this couple spends little time together, each person being very active with friends from the same sex. He wants to spend time with the boys but expects her to take care of the house and be responsible; she wants to spend time with the girls, but expects *him* to take care of the house and be responsible. Each becomes jealous over the other's friends and tries to limit her or his involvement with them.

Another telling clue of this particular interactional style has to do with how the couple deals with conflict: the most usual method is flight. When they disagree—when each tries to get the other to do what he or she wants and fails—the battle is carried out by leaving. One or the other leaves the relationship to go to his or her mother, father, or friends, or simply to run away.

A third striking clue of this particular relationship is the manner in which the partners deal with each other prior to leaving in conflict. Generally speaking, this couple has a great deal of action. They fight, they hit each other, they tear up each other's clothes, they throw things out the window, they behave like children. In fact, this couple has a penchant for involving other people in the community in their struggle, including police, courts, pastors, parents, and neighbors. They are very much like two children who get into a fight; when the fight gets dirty, the parents (actual or metaphorical) step in and try to separate them.

The Therapeutic Relationship

Bob and Martha, both 27 years old, grew up together in a small midwestern town. They were neighbors and classmates all through school. In junior high, Martha decided that Bob would be her husband, so she pursued him with a vengeance. When Bob told Martha that his parents would not allow him to date, Martha went over to have a talk with them and changed their minds. Later, when Bob and Martha graduated from high school and she had entered nursing school, Martha announced to his and her parents that she and Bob would be getting married when she finished training. As Bob predicted, his parents objected, but Martha was able to sway them, especially since Bob suffered from a lot of physical problems (hay fever, back problems, and some addictive issues around food and alcohol) and could benefit from "good nursing care." Bob, who went to work at his father's gas station right after high school, saved his money and continued to live at home. The courtship consisted of his visiting Martha at school and her occasional attendance when Bob was hospitalized for various ailments (1981 for back surgery, 1983 for chemical addiction). Martha spent the early years of the marriage "coaching" Bob on how to comb his hair, develop his latent musical talents (the tuba), correct his posture, dress appropriately, and enroll in college (Fall of 1991). During these early years, Martha though it best not to have children. The crushing realization that Bob had grown up and was involved in a gay relationship pushed Martha into depression and a suicide attempt in late 1992. Bob, who had filed for divorce a month earlier and moved in with his lover, agreed to try to work out the marriage. Bob's lover was subsequently diagnosed as HIV positive.

SII: Therapeutic Relationship

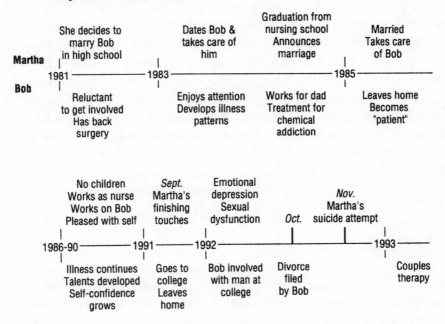

Description

The therapeutic relationship is a system in which each person tries to behave as if he or she is the doctor and other is the patient: he tries to help her, and she tries to help him.

The difficulty with this relationship is that each person becomes a member of the older generation while simultaneously becoming a member of the younger generation; they very rarely function as adults with each other. Each most often functions as a parent to the other, taking responsibility for and charge of the other person.

Predictable Pattern Clues

When beginning the SII of this relationship, this particular couple pattern will frequently stand out in the early courtship process. Usually at the time the couple were courting, each of them was experiencing some difficulty in life. Perhaps he was having difficulty holding a job; perhaps she was having difficulty separating from her parents. Thus, at the point of dating, each person began to take responsibility for improving the other person's situation in life. Each thus becomes the other's doctor, trying to treat the other person's problems.

The difficulty in the relationship is that each person becomes confined to his or her role. Thus, the doctor becomes frustrated because the patient either will not get well or is getting well too fast. In contrast, the patient becomes distressed because the doctor will not treat him or her, or because that person still does try to treat him or her.

The Pseudorelationship

Brenda, age 47, and James, age 52, are both well-educated professionals. She is a practicing physician, and he is a partner in a wealthy law firm. They met in graduate school in 1969 and found that they shared cultural and musical interests. Given the taxing nature of their studies, the free time spent together was "divine." An occasional weekend away, ski trips, and good food with fine wine capped their mutual interest. A pregnancy followed by a quiet abortion in 1970 gave them pause to continue their commitment and future. After some therapy regarding depression following the abortion, they decided to get married in 1972. One child, Michael, was born in 1974. Over the years, both Brenda and James have reached the top in their specialties and have found their enjoyment in professional and in civic activities. Currently, they have become anxious about the marriage, and recently affairs by both of them have prompted therapy. Both adore their son (who in 1991 began studying at a distant university) and want to preserve the marriage for the sake of the family.

SII: Pseudorelationship

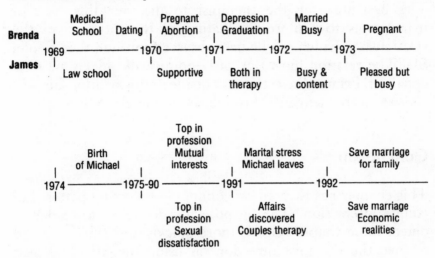

Description

The pseudorelationship is one without commitment. To put it in other terms, some people have a wedding, but never get married. Theirs is a relationship that lacks intimacy, a relationship in which the bonding process never quite took place. Bonding problems in couple relationships have many origins. Perhaps one of the most common problems relates to pregnancy prior to commitment. There are some couples in which a pregnancy occurs and the couple goes ahead and has the wedding (but, as noted, never really gets married). Sometimes we colloquially say, "it is the baby who had the wedding, not the couple." Even though the couple may live together for years, a careful examination will indicate that the temperature in the relationship is very cool.

In some marriages, each person is already "married" to

somebody or something else. An example of this kind of marriage would be the situation in which one or both spouses are heavily invested in their own careers, and the marriage is purely secondary.

Predictable Pattern Clues

The best way for the therapist to discover this type of marriage is to explore the nature of the intimacy in the relationship, which can be best observed through the use of a SII. The relationship's lack of bonding will quickly become apparent. Primary investments outside of this relationship will also be easily identified through the use of the SII.

Conclusion

This chapter has focused on commonly recurring patterns of couple interaction. The purpose was to help the reader to detect some couple systems more quickly and efficiently and to give the therapist direction on using the SII. The next chapter will outline some of our major areas of focus, some sample questions, and what we are looking for. (Obviously, this is a rather difficult task; it is not easy to put in static written from the flexibility and fluidity of the SII.) We will also provide a more specific diagram to use when conducting an SII.

4

Exploring the Territory:
A Guideline for the Structured
Initial Interview

This chapter will offer an outline for the therapist's first meetings with a couple and the subsequent process of evaluation and information-gathering sessions of the SII. It is meant to be a reference for the therapist in his or her work with the couple in the evaluation process: the SII by its nature allows for much flexibility in style, pace, areas of focus, rhythm, and content. The suggested questions (and others) will be placed in the context of a couple and explored in greater detail in Chapter 5.

Dyadic Questioning

Before we look at specific questions, it is important to introduce the reader to a specific technique in our questioning process called *dyadic questioning*. This is a process whereby the therapist asks one partner questions about the other, especially when the therapist wants to elicit information (thoughts, feelings, beliefs, ideas, or fantasies) about nodal aspects of the couple's relationship (That is, significant psychological events or aspects of their relationship, or interpretive aspects of their history together as a couple). By asking one partner about the other's behaviors, attitudes, or emotions, the therapist not only forces the couple to expand their thinking process about the relationship but also places himself or herself in a meta position to the couple. This dyadic questioning style keeps the focus systemic and forces the couple to think relationally.

The SII, when conducted with large doses of dyadic questioning, forces the couple to fit together pieces of their own puzzle. This constant feedback into the couple's system pushes them to explore their complex relationship and their perceptions of it.

Dyadic Questioning Targets

There are three significant areas of focus for the dyadic questions. Some questions are targeted at eliciting feedback about *similarity and dissimilarity*. Many couples evolve a mythology saying that they are very different from each other, when to the outside observer it appears that the couple operates on very similar psychological levels with regard to maturity, self-esteem, and the like. A therapist, therefore, when exploring the first date can say something like, "Mary, when you got back to your dormitory room and your roommate said to you, 'How did you like John,' what did you say?" or, "How was John different from the other guys you dated?"

Other questions are targeted at gathering specific information about *couple interaction*. For example, if John became angry with Mary during the early dating period for dating another guy, the therapist could ask Mary: "How did you explain John's anger? What did you think it was about? What was he wanting you to do? What did he do with his anger?" And, looking at John, the therapist could ask: "What was Mary up to? How did you explain it to yourself? What was she trying to say to you?"

Still other questions are targeted at gathering further information about *nodal events or historical "hiccups"* that caused conflict and/or trauma to the couple. For example, when examining the couple's decision to get married after the woman found out she was pregnant, the therapist could ask: "John, what did you think Mary really wanted to do? Do you think that both her head and her heart were together in wanting to go ahead with the wedding?" The therapist could ask the same or similar questions to the other partner. The key is to target the dyadic questions to expand the couple's thinking process concerning the ideas they had previously formed about the events.

Eye Contact

When using dyadic questioning, it is important for the therapist to be conscious of eye contact and head placement. When looking at and talking to John about Mary, for example, the therapist's eyes and head must face toward John, or Mary will likely try to interrupt the process. Nonverbal focus is important in being able to use the dyadic questioning process successfully.

Directive and Nondirective Questions About Nodal Events

It is also important to remember that there are two types of questioning styles when exploring nodal events. *Directive questions* are questions directed to one of the partners because the therapist either wants to balance the interaction by having the quieter partner talk or desires specific information from one partner.

Nondirective questions are questions that are directed to either partner. When using nondirective questions, it is important for the therapist to look between the couple or away from them entirely so as not to give some subtle clue as to which partner should speak first. This form of questioning is for the purpose of seeing which partner will initiate the response and allows the therapist the opportunity to make inferences about the structure and power distribution of the relationship.

Dyadic Questions and the SII

Many of the questions in this chapter are written in a straight monadic form, as if directed to each partner. It is very difficult to write an entire chapter in the dyadic questioning style, partly because teaching the SII requires an alternating focus between *nodal events* that need to be explored and *interactional processes* that need to be discovered. Despite the monadic style of some of the following questions, however, a therapist should use the dyadic questioning style as much as possible.

Remarriage and the SII

When working with a couple where one or both partners have previously cohabited or been married, we suggest that therapists conduct the SII on the current relationship first. After concluding the SII, but before the wrap-up, conduct a brief SII on any previous relationship. If a therapist focuses on a previous relationship first, we believe it is often received negatively by the couple. In addition, when the therapist has completed the SII on the current relationship, he or she has an idea of the kinds of unresolved themes that might appear in the SII on any previous relationship.

When conducting an SII on a previous relationship, the therapist need not necessarily go into as much detail as for the current relationship. The therapist might, for example, in surveying the time before the birth of the first child, simply ask the couple about conflictual issues during those three years, rather than taking each third of the three years separately. The more SIIs a therapist has conducted, the easier it will be to condense the SIIs of any previous relationships and yet find those unresolved themes that are being brought forward into the current relationship.

Creating the Contract

Introduction of Self to Couple

- Identify their preferred names
- Identify referral source.

Identify Family Constellation

- Are you presently living together? Are you separated?
- Do you have children; if so, are they in the home or out?
- How long have you been a couple?
- What do each of you do for employment?

Identify Presenting Problem

- What brought you here today?
- How do you each see the problems? (Discuss this briefly, balancing the timing and interaction.)

Identify Precipitating Event (This is a good assessment clue.)

- Why did you decide to come in now? Why not six months ago or two years ago?
- What are you hiring me to do?

Attempted Solutions/Previous Therapy

- What have you tried on your own to solve these issues?
- Have you had previous therapy? Was the therapy individual or couple?

- What did you learn in your previous therapy? What helped? (Avoid making same analysis as previous therapist.)

Negotiating the SII

If you as the therapist have now determined that the couple is ready and willing to do the SII, it can now be proposed and explained. (See page 15 in Chapter 2.)

Exploring Courtship

You may find it rather unusual that we give such careful attention to the dating relationship of a couple. For married couples, we often spend more time on the dating relationship, proportionately, than on the years of marital relationship. The same is true for cohabiting couples; we often spend more time on the period prior to living together than on the period afterward.

The reason we spend so much time on the early experiences is our assumption that at the point of commitment, the partners needed each other. This is a way of saying that we believe committed relationships are not accidental. The question running through our minds is, "Why did this woman (or man) pick this person out of all the millions of men (or women) in the world?" Our search for the answer has a twofold purpose:

1. To give the couple some awareness of their special relationship (that is, their system) and how they carved it out
2. To give the therapist some understanding of the scope and nature of the relationship

In short, the reason that we spend time trying to understand the early phase of the relationship is because this is when the rules, roles, and rituals of the couple began.

First Meeting

- When did the two of you meet? What year was it? How old were each of you at the time? (Use the board or newsprint to chart the answers to these questions.)
- How did you first meet? Did you know each other before you met?
- Who introduced you? What do you remember about your first meeting?

First Impressions

- If you had a best friend to whom you told everything, and he or she said, "What did you think of [name of partner] after you got back from your first date, what would you have said?
- What did you like about [name of partner]?
- What attracted you to him (or her)? What ways did you think you were similar?
- What did you discover about him (or her) that was different, unusual, or strange?

Second Date

- How long after the first meeting did the second date occur?
- Who initiated it?
- Where did you go, and how did you decide what you were going to do on the date?

Second Impressions

- At the end of the second date, what did you find attractive about the other person?

- Did you discover anything else that was unusual, different or strange? (Remember to use dyadic questions.)

Family/Friends Response
- How did your friends respond to you dating the other person?
- What did they like about the other person? What didn't they like?

Exclusivity/Inclusivity
- Did you continue to date others? Was the dating of others discussed?
- When did you decide to stop dating others? If you stopped dating others without discussing it, when did you begin to know or sense that the other person was no longer interested in other people?
- If you discussed the subject and decided not to date other people, how did this discussion go? When did it occur?

Steady Dating
- When did each of you see yourself as going together or "steady"? (Again, remember to use dyadic questions.)
- How did you arrive at the decision? Did you discuss it, or did it just happen?
- What did friends think of your commitment to go steady?
- What did your parents think?
- When did you say to yourself, "He (or she) is for me," or "He (or she) is someone I'd marry?" (that is, when did you make an internal commitment?).

Separations
- When the two of you went your separate ways for the summer, what did you say about the relationship? Where did you think [name of other person] was in regard to the

relationship? How would you each have defined the relationship at that point in time?

External Commitment

- When did you begin to say to the other, "You're for me," or "I could see us getting married," or "I'd like to be with you forever," or "I could see myself marrying you?" (that is, when did you make an external commitment?).

Engagement

- Did you discuss getting engaged? Was it a surprise? When did you become engaged? Did you tell others? Did you make a public announcement?
- How did you parents react to the engagement? Did you inform them or request their permission?

Conflict

- Did you have any arguments?
- How often did you argue?
- What issues or concerns caused arguments?
- How did you make sense out of those arguments?
- How were the arguments resolved?
- Who initiated the peacemaking or making-up effort?
- What was the relationship like after you made up?

Communication Behaviors

- How did you know if you said or did something [name of partner] didn't like?
- How did you know if you said or did something that pleased [name of partner]?

Family of Origin

- In what way is the other person's handling of anger similar to that of his (or her) father?
- In what way is the other person's handling of anger similar to that of his (or her) mother?
- In what way is the other person's handling of affection similar to that of his (or her) father?
- In what way is the other person's handling of affection similar to that of his (or her) mother?

Affection and Sex

- How did you know [name of partner] was happy with you?
- Did he (or she) tell you? Show you by behavior?
- How do each of you demonstrate nongenital affection?
- Where along the courtship/dating/engagement process did you become sexually involved? Before or after getting married?
- Who initiated it? Did you discuss it first?
- How did you experience it? Was it positive? Were you anxious or negative about it?
- What pattern did your sexual relationship take? How often did you have sex?
- Were you both satisfied with the sexual relationship then?
- What about now? Who initiates it? (Check frequency.)
- Have you ever noticed [name of partner] having arousal problems?

Reaction to Engagement

- How did your family react to the engagement?
- How did you see the other person's father reacting to the engagement?

- How did you see the other person's mother reacting to the engagement?

Planning the Wedding

- How did you see your partner's mother's involvement with planning the wedding?
- How did you see your partner's father's involvement with planning the wedding?
- Were there any problems with the wedding plans?

For some couples the distance between the engagement and the wedding is relatively short, and thus they are very involved in planning the wedding as soon as the engagement or intention to marry is announced. Other couples have a relatively long period of time between the engagement and the wedding; thus, the planning of the wedding does not take place until several months have passed after the engagement.

Commitment: The Glue of Relationships

All these questions and many more are part of the exploration of the relationship history. It has been our experience that these questions are necessary to give us clues to understanding the rhythm of the couple's relationship and the consequences for their present interaction pattern.

We make an assumption that an intimate relationship is a unique phenomenon, and that it involves a particular kind of bonding that we refer to as *commitment*. This commitment takes place on many levels, involving the whole person and a lengthy span of time.

During the evaluation of the early phase, we are concerned about the nature of the bonding process within the couple. Generally speaking, the commitment process begins internally when each person in the relationship says to himself or herself about the other, "You are for me." The second step in this process is dyadic and external, as each person makes this same statement to the other verbally and nonverbally. The third step in the commitment process is a public one, when the couple announces their bonding to the world.

Some relationship struggles have their origin in the faulty or fraudulent bonding process. For example, some couples, despite their wedding, never have a marriage. From the very beginning, their relationship is cool; rather than having a true marriage, they have a pseudomarriage or a nonmarriage.

Other couples have difficulty with the bonding process in regard to becoming exclusive. This can be related to many factors, including the inability to deal openly with differences, negativity, and anger. The bonding thus occurs in a peculiar way and may continue as a struggle after cohabitation or the wedding. By examining the bonding process, the therapist will also receive some clues as to other peculiar kinds of bonding.

Predictable Relationship Themes

Dependency

It has been our experience that certain themes appear over and over again in couple therapy populations. One of these themes has to do with dependency needs and the inability of partners to fulfill them (see Chapter 3).

By careful examination of the courtship process, a therapist develops hints and clues about the dependency needs of both partners and how they handled them. For example, the speed with which the bonding takes place may have something to do with the dependency levels of the partners. Sometimes very dependent people meet and move together very quickly, talking about marriage or a life commitment on the first date and living together by the end of the first week.

How individuals handle their dependency needs also can

been seen during these early phases. People who experience their dependency needs as significant very rarely can talk about them. Usually they despise the dependent part of their personality and thus avoid talking about it and/or cover their dependency needs with a quality of rebelliousness, irritation, or anger. Silence and aloofness is another favorite technique for people who want to appear strong even though they feel weak on the inside.

Self-Esteem

Another theme that appears frequently in clinical populations has to do with self-esteem. Couples who have difficulties with self-esteem have a great deal of trouble handling differences of opinions. During the early dating process, they usually act as though they think, feel, believe, and fantasize in exactly the same manner. Arguments are avoided at all costs. Each partner feels the need to be loved by the other and, thus, does not wish to threaten the prospect of being loved because of a disagreement. The dating experiences of couples with low self-esteem therefore are often remarkably calm and peaceful. Couples with good self-esteem deal with differences of opinions and have disagreements and arguments in an attempt to arrive at mutually satisfying solutions.

Even though couples with low self-esteem experience differences, they usually camouflage them. Therefore, it is important when looking at the dating relationship to ask each partner not only what he or she found out about the other that was different or unusual, but also how he or she went about to plan a program to change that other person.

All of this is a way of saying that couples with low self-esteem often have a great deal of difficulty with fusion or enmeshment. These couples believe that living together should be a state of perfect togetherness where they see, think, feel, and dream identically. When they discover differences, each attempts to change the other person to bring about a state of oneness.

Power/Shape

An exploration of the dating relationship will also give the therapist some sense about how the relationship was set up and who accepted it. The therapist will thus be able to obtain some clues regarding the complimentary or symmetrical quality of the relationship. In addition, careful questioning of the couple will enable the therapist to obtain information about the struggle for power in this relationship, including who is in charge and what the covert and overt rules are for power and the inflicting of pain.

After the Public Commitment

The following are topical areas of focus that can be checked and monitored in the chronological journey through the marriage. Depending on the length of the marriage, years can be divided up into seasons, thirds, or halves. We most often use thirds: Christmas to Memorial Day, Memorial Day to Labor Day, and Labor Day to Christmas. Our basic concern is exploring the years of the marriage or cohabitation relationship (which we usually do on a year-by-year basis) is to develop a sense of the rhythm of the relationship.

Some marriage and committed relationships change and shift over the years; we are interested in noting the movement. This can be most clearly conceptualized in terms of intimacy or closeness. Sometimes couples are working on getting closer—heating up the relationship, so to speak, or making a bid for greater intimacy. In contrast, some couples are attempting to increase their distance and/or are working on other agendas. Other couples develop a kind of lock in their relationship. It is as though the relationship has become dead; they can neither come closer nor get away from each other.

Once again, we want to remind potential users that the SII is a flexible tool. Therapists can add or delete areas based on their own perspectives of relationships and their own perceptivity. Although we conduct the SII generally on a year-by-year basis, we do so always with a concern to avoid getting bogged down. If the therapist enters an area of unresolved conflict, he or she should briefly examine the parameters of the conflict and move on. Do not think the conflict can be solved in this portion of the contract; continue to search for themes and rhythms.

Generally speaking, we use the themes or areas of focus in a chronological fashion, looking at each of them in a year-by-year fashion. Sometimes, however, we telescope the years because some couples have little going on; it stays the same year after year. At other times, we form composites, looking at specific areas of focus during the whole duration of the marriage. For example, one might look at all of the pregnancies, comparing and contrasting them in terms of how they were experienced by the wife and husband and of the effect of each child on the relationship.

In the case of a relationship of long duration, we assign homework after the first session. Now that the couple are familiar with what we are looking for, we give them the task of preparing themselves for the next session by going over the material in advance.

The pacing of the SII is dependent upon the couple involved. For couples that have not previously discussed such difficult issues as sexuality, in-laws, anger, affection, and parenting, the therapist may want to move more slowly through the SII and gather very detailed information and impressions. Process value can be increased by the therapist thoroughly exploring the perceptions, responses, and interpretations of each mate regarding problem issues or events. For lengthier marriages (15 years or more), the therapist may move briskly at times and focus closely on problem issues or crisis periods. Again, the adaptability of this assessment tool to the needs of the couple is the key element to its value.

Many of the following questions are focused on significant events in the life of a couple, events that often become points of conflict or different interpretations. Remember that all of the areas below should be explored using the dyadic questioning style as frequently as possible.

Weddings

- How did the wedding plans develop? Was there any interference from her parents? From his parents?
- How did each of you experience the wedding?
- As you were planning the honeymoon, how did you arrive at the decision to do whatever you did?

Honeymoon

- How did the honeymoon go? Did it meet each of your expectations?
- Were there any conflicts during the honeymoon? How did you resolve them?

Social Life

- How did the two of you handle your social life prior to the wedding? Did each of you have friends apart from the other person? Were some friends dropped along the way?
- When did the two of you begin to establish friends as a couple that were not known to each of you individually before you started seeing each other?

Social Planning

- Who was in charge of the social calendar? Did one or both of you initiate ideas regarding your social life?
- When asked to do something, did you need to check with the other person first?
- If you both were asked to engage in some activity and one partner was sick but not seriously ill, could or did the other go alone?

Finances

- How did you decide to handle finances?
- Who banked the money? Who wrote the checks? Did the two of you have separate checking accounts or a joint account?
- Was the arrangement the two of you decided upon similar or identical to that followed in either of your families of origin?
- Are there problems in this arrangement?
- Did any financial crisis (such as job loss, layoff, or business failure) occur? What was its effect?

A reminder: the financial area needs to be checked year by year; thus, this question needs to be asked periodically during the time line. Sometimes couples give you a clue by indicating that they had one arrangement at the beginning of the marriage and then a different one ten years later. If so, then you can ask about the financial restructuring later.

Sexuality

- (to her) Did you notice whether he had any difficulty in achieving or maintaining an erection at the onset of the marriage?
- (to her) Did you notice whether he had a tendency to ejaculate prematurely?
- (to him) did you notice whether she had any orgasmic difficulties?
- What was the frequency of intercourse at the onset of the marriage—too often, too rare, just right?

Vocation/Education

- Check career development of each person.
- If one of the two does not work outside the home, how was that decided?

- Are work hours/schedules causing conflict?
- Is work triangulated into the marriage?
- Did a work/business/employment crisis cause abnormal stress on the couple?

Residence Changes/Moves

- Do you rent, or are you buying a house?
- (if buying) How was the decision made to buy a house?
- How was the location decided?
- What concerns did you have regarding these decisions?

Pregnancy

- How was it decided to have children?
- (to him) How did she respond as her body began to change and grow larger?
- (to her) How did he respond to your changing body?
- Were there any difficulties during the pregnancy?
- How were the difficulties handled or resolved?

Children

- What changes occurred after the birth of each child?
- How were the parenting responsibilities assigned and arranged?
- Did you have concerns regarding the parenting of the other person?
- Did you have questions regarding your own parenting?
- Did you believe that the other person was too easy or too hard?
- Did both of you agree on how to parent? Were you a team?

In-Laws/Families of Origin

- Check relationships throughout, especially in crisis periods.
- Is one mate seen as too involved with his or her family?
- Explore changes as a result of family-of-origin crises (such as death, divorce, illnesses, or financial problems).
- Does an in-law interfere? How? What is done about it?
- Does the couple seem to be involved in a chronic struggle over whose family "blueprint" to follow?
- Are that any social class conflicts?
- Are there any struggles over religious issues?
- Are there any racial or cultural struggles?

Anger

- Is anger expressed directly, verbally, behaviorally? Is it forced underground?
- Is anger expressed through attacking behaviors? Through withdrawal?
- How do you know when the other person is angry?
- Who wins? Who makes up?
- Check throughout for changes in frequency of conflict.
- What are the most common issues of conflict? (Don't get too bogged down in content).
- Are they pseudohostile (that is, do they fight to get closer?)
- Do they make love by fighting?
- Do they fight to get distance?
- Do they think that married couples are not supposed to fight?

Substance Abuse

- Monitor any development of increased, problematic, or abusive use of alcohol, drugs, or food

- Is this a distancing mechanism? Expression of anger?
- Also check for compulsive exercising or jogging, as these can be distancing mechanisms.

Affairs/Triangulation

- Are there, or were there, any romantic affairs or social liaisons?
- In each case where one occurred, was it an effort to heat up the relationship or to maintain distance?
- Are one or both parents aligned with a partner in the couple, perpetuating a relationship that is emotionally more intimate than the marriage?
- Does the marriage need the presence of a third party, like an in-law or a friend who lives with the couple?
- Do hobbies, activities, work, or friends act as an "affair"?

Fusion/Symbiosis

- How stuck together are the couple?
- Does each seem overly dependent on the other making him or her happy?
- How do they tolerate differences in thoughts, feelings, and behavior of the other?
- Is all their energy going into the relationship?

Dependency

- Does one mate allow abnormal domination and control by the other?
- Does the other want abnormal control?
- Is one mate overly dependent on the other making decisions?
- Does the other mate need to be depended upon like this?

Self-Esteem

- Does each or either partner have unrealistically high expectations?
- Does each or either always expect the worst?
- Is one partner robbing the other to feel good? Is the other being robbed to look good or validate himself or herself? (This indicates a therapeutic relationship.)
- Do they have great difficulty asking for what they want?
- Can they express anger appropriately?
- Are they overly sensitive to conflict and thus avoid it, or do they attack so that they will not be attacked or have to express their vulnerability?
- Does each have elaborate dreams that do not match reality and thus cause much pain?

Again you will notice that we ask many questions, but with a sense of timing in historical development. Many of the questions are raised again and again; the basic themes of decision making, power plays, intimacy, and distancing factors are searched for. In fact, we can best describe our experience with the SII as that of weaving a tapestry. We are concerned with weaving together how the couple developed their relationship, how they each helped it along, and how they each helped build their system of interaction. Thus, we want to know how Helen helped Al with his drinking, how Al helped Helen with her affair, and so forth. Sometimes couples experience the SII as very therapeutic, and it alone gets the job done without further work. Nonetheless, the therapist is setting the stage for a drama with a cast of characters that has already been screen-tested, has been properly cued regarding the script, and is immune from stage fright.

As we see it, couples carve out, maintain, and defend their systems. The purpose of examining the years of the whole relationship is to make the couple more aware of the bilateral quality of their relationship, the manner in which each of them helped carve out and develop the patterns. In using the SII, we are essentially in search of the relationship system, trying to get some sense of the couple's interaction. The real dilemma for both therapist and clients is whether or not to continue with the assessment. The next chapter will provide a case study using the SII assessment technique.

5
Understanding the Terrain: Illustrating the Structured Initial Interview

J ust as if the map is not the territory, the SII most certainly is not the whole relationship. Like the map, however, the SII can be helpful in predicting appropriate directions. Working with couples is really an opportunity not only to explore their history and understanding of their choices, but also to clarify their decisions. If the couple have been traveling over terrain that has been emotionally, physically, and economically exhausting, allowing them to rest awhile in the therapist's office might be an apt metaphor for exploring their relational map through the use of the SII.

In the following case history, we will follow a couple from their early dating years to their current situation. The reader will notice the case history is on the left and will unfold as the questions from the SII which appear on the right side, are asked. The questions will reflect the history of the couple as presented. More details on the use of questions and specific questions pertaining to different phases of the history of a couple can be found in Chapter 3.

The reader will also notice that the graphics of the SII will appear on the right. These graphics present the information that both the therapist and couple will see. The genogram at the beginning is one other way of helping to gather and simplify family-of-origin data. Although many of the questions used with John and Mary (our sample couple) are written in a monadic style, do not forget that the effectiveness of the SII will largely be determined by the use of dyadic questioning, as discussed in Chapter 4.

Table 5–1 on pages 92 and 93 will pull together all of the data that has been developed in the smaller, partial graphs on the preceding pages, presenting a total view of the SII gathered during the initial interviews.

Case History

Mary, age thirty-seven, and John, age thirty-six, were married in August of 1977 and have three children living at home: Patrick, age ten, Mark, age six, and Lisa, age one. Their first child, John Jr., died shortly after birth. Currently, Mary is employed as an office manager, and John is a sales representative. Mary is the youngest of two children; her older brother is now divorced. Mary's parents have been married for forty years and still live in the first house they purchased. John is the oldest of four children; he has a brother, who is one year younger, and two sisters, who are four and six years younger. His father died in 1985, and his mother remarried in 1989 and lives nearby.

Marital and Family Constellation Questions

- Are you presently living together?
- Are you separated or divorced?
- Do you have children in or out of home?
- What is the length of this marriage?
- What do each of you do for employment?

Genogram Format

SII Format

1977	78	82	85	86	89	91	92	Feb.
Married	Death of son	Birth of Patrick	Death of John's father	Birth of Mark	John's mother remarries	Birth of Lisa		Couples therapy

Case History

Both John and Mary are in agreement about coming to therapy, which they see as a place to talk about a problem in their marriage. John perceives Mary as uninterested in a sexual relationship with him; she has "forced" him to move out of the bedroom. Mary, who admits to being uninterested in sex, claims that John's most recent affair (during this past year) was the reason. John and Mary are concerned about the future direction of their marriage, not only for the sake of the children, but for themselves as well. The therapist has come recommended as one who can save marriages.

Case History

Both John and Mary have been to see therapists before; the first time was in 1978, right after their baby died. Usually the therapy has helped, but the last therapist, in 1985, told Mary that she should get out of the relationship. This blunt assessment scared her. John saw Mary's therapist for a few sessions, just to get Mary off his back. His seeing the therapist seemed to quiet the tension in the marriage as well as to help his own depression. John and Mary both agreed that the baby's death affected their marital relationship and that their sexual relationship became strained as a result. They sought therapy as a couple in 1981, as well as in 1985, when John was depressed as a result of his father's death.

Presenting Problem Questions

- What brought you here today?
- How do you each see the problems? (Discuss briefly, balancing the time between each partner.)
- Identify precipitating event (a good assessment clue).
- Why did you decide to come in now? Why not before?
- What are you hiring me to do?

SII

Attempted Solutions/Previous Therapy Questions

- What have you tried on your own to solve these issues?
- Have you had any previous therapy? Individual, conjoint, or family?
- What did you learn in your previous therapy? What helped? What was not helpful?

SII

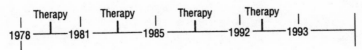

Case History

John was born in 1957 and raised in Chicago. Prior to graduating from high school in 1975, he had a rather extensive dating pattern. His involvement with a high school classmate resulted in a pregnancy and an abortion; his family (made up of traditional Roman Catholics) was not told of either. During his first years at the University of Iowa, he frequently dated girls for short periods of time. He was not interested in getting "hooked," and usually he was the one who broke off the relationships. Mary was born in a rural town of church-going Methodists in Iowa in 1956. Her dating prior to graduating from high school in 1974 was minimal; the boy she had dated was killed in Vietnam. She worked for one year after high school before entering the University of Iowa in 1975. She had no prior sexual experience before meeting John.

They met while taking an economics class when they were both sophomores in the fall of 1976. Mary thought John was handsome, witty, devilish, and very sexy; he liked her homey style and her naturalness. It surprised him somewhat when she asked him out for a cup of coffee.

The first date was in the student union. Mary sensed John wanted more than coffee, but she suggested only that they get together again in a week. John called her that night and every night prior to the next date. On that night, after a movie and pizza, John asked Mary to go dancing. Mary declined, saying she had some exams to prepare for; John's drinking and sexual advances had also made her uneasy. She said to call her in a week. He called the next day.

Initial Acquaintance Questions

- How did you first meet? Did you know each other before?
- Who introduced you? What do you remember about your first meeting?
- What were your first impressions? What did you like about the other person? What did you dislike? (Things they initially like are often things they dislike later.)
- What attracted you? Why him or her and not someone else?
- How did the first date occur? How long was this after the first meeting?
- Who initiated it?
- Where did you go? What did you do?
- What did you learn about the other person as a result of the second date?
- How soon was the next date? Why did you want another date?

SII

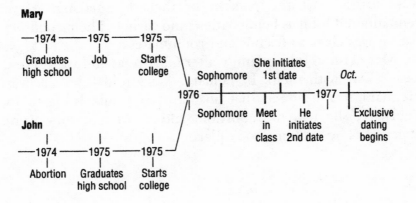

Case History

John's persistence in calling pushed up the third date to the next evening. "Just [going] out for coffee" was the way they both described the time together. Mary still had the feeling that John was rushing toward greater affection, and she was put off by his saying that "there are plenty of fish in the sea." By October 1976, however, they were dating each other exclusively. At one point, Mary saw John holding hands with another woman. When confronted, John said they were "old friends," and that it was nothing serious. He promised not to see other women as "dates."

At Thanksgiving, John accompanied Mary to her family home. Her parents liked John, and even though he was Catholic, they all attended a Methodist church together. When they returned to campus, they talked of marriage and the future. On the following weekend, they slept together for the first time. Even though Mary was shy and a virgin, John was surprised at the passion of their lovemaking. Mary remembered John as being patient and caring. Their exclusive dating was clear to friends and roommates.

Mary visited John's family after Christmas and spent New Year's Day with them. In January, Mary told John she was pregnant. Both agreed that an abortion would be best. In February, she had the abortion, and in March, they were engaged. The wedding took place in August of 1977.

Dating Pattern/Rhythm Questions

- How often did you date? Once a week? Twice a week? Daily?
- Were you each also dating other people when you first dated?
- When did it become exclusive?
- What was the rhythmic pattern?
- How did family/friends respond to your dating?
- Were there school, work, or other conflicts?
- Any breakups or forced separations? (Highly dependent couples often establish torrid dating patterns and have quick courtships and/or frequent and dramatic breakups.)

SII

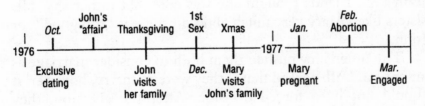

Case History

Given the rush to make decisions regarding the pregnancy in January 1977, both John and Mary struggled with guilt regarding the abortion. Their decision to begin a sexual relationship was based on a perceived commitment after John's promise not to see other women and John and Mary's visit to her parents at Thanksgiving.

Mary felt she was always attracted to John from their first meeting, but was fearful of rushing their relationship. She turned down other offers to date in early October 1976. Even though there were differences in geographical (small town versus city), religious (Protestant versus Catholic) and ethnic (German versus Italian) backgrounds, she felt they were a perfect match.

John liked Mary from the start. He was surprised at her limits early in the relationship, but grew to respect the no-sex rule that she insisted on in their initial dating. His parents liked Mary and thought she would offer stability for John. John's old friends thought she was cute, but rather shy. His sisters liked Mary very much and said she was "too good" for John.

The pregnancy pushed them both to consider marriage as an option. Both agreed that if they were to marry, however, it should not be a forced decision. After the abortion, they remained sexually inactive until they decided to get engaged in March 1977. Though their families and friends were surprised, John and Mary planned an August wedding before returning to the university.

Bonding Process Questions

- When did you see yourselves as going steady?
- How did you define it to yourself?
- How did others see you?
- What did your family think? (Check differentiation.)
- When did you say to yourself, "He (or she) is for me," or "He (or she) is someone I'd marry (that is, make an internal commitment)?
- When did you begin to say this to the other person (that is, make an external commitment)?
- When were you definitely serious?
- Did you discuss getting engaged, or was it a surprise? When did you become engaged (that is, make a public commitment)? How long was the engagement?

SII

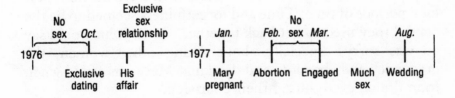

Case History

There has been little change over the years in terms of arguments and the expression of anger: John tends to blow up when he does not get his way, and Mary tends to go silent. Perhaps the differences in temperament or ethnic background feed into this. Mary sees John as demanding and unrelenting when he wants something. He hates her "clamming up"; she hates his octopus-like clinging and smothering. Arguments often are about how or whose needs are more important.

When Mary confronted John about going out with other women during the courtship, John was hurt that she did not trust him. John views Mary as steady and calm to the point of being boring. He was used to fighting things out in his family and finds Mary's family closed and nonpassionate. A lot of John's discontent revolves around Mary's unwillingness to forgive him for getting angry, which he believes is acting "like it is some kind of sin to be human." Mary views John's anger as a sign of immaturity and a lack of control. She was very surprised when he would blow up and then leave the house for long periods of time. Time and forgetfulness seemed to be the "cure" they used to get back together. Often John would say he was sorry, especially about dating other women, the pregnancy and abortion, and drinking. Mary was afraid when John drank, even during their courtship.

Conflict Questions

- When did the arguments begin? How often did you argue? How did you express your anger?
- What issues or concerns caused an argument?
- What didn't you like about the other person? What did you see as unusual, different, or strange?
- How did you know when he or she was angry?
- How did you resolve it? Who initiated making up?

SII

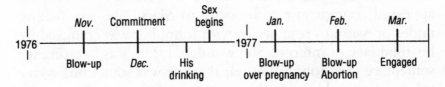

Case History

Sexual behavior has been a source of conflict for John and Mary. From the very beginning of their courtship, Mary said John was looking for sex, whereas she was looking for intimacy. An agreement about sex seemed to occur after John promised not to see other women and after the joint visit to Mary's parents and their approval of John. The sexual relationship was new to Mary, and she relied on John to be gentle and knowledgeable. She had never been "unhappy with sex," but needed to experience it in the context of intimacy and safety. John, while being a very tactile person, was also a very "hurried guy" and did not like to "wait all night." In many ways, John initiated the requests for sex, whereas Mary was the one who gave permission.

In John's view, it was Mary's job to not get pregnant before marriage. Getting pregnant was "her fault," said John, and a way to keep him "locked into the relationship." After the abortion, John seemed unable to have sex; instead, he appeared content just to be close to Mary. She was feeling under pressure to resume sex with John, but was confused by his total lack of interest. She wondered if he was "getting it" someplace else. John often felt that sex was something Mary tolerated, and that with the exception of the first few weeks, she rarely was orgasmic. Both agreed that the fear of another pregnancy made sex an anxious experience.

Affection and Sex Questions

- How did you each show nonsexual affection?
- How did you know the other person was happy with you?
- Did he or she tell you? Show you by behavior?
- Where in the courtship/dating/engagement process did you become sexually involved?
- Who initiated it? Did you discuss it first?
- Was it experienced as positive? Were you anxious or negative about it?
- How often did you have intercourse? What pattern did it take?
- Were you both satisfied with the sexual relationship then?
- What about now? Who initiates it? (Check frequency.)
- Have you ever noticed your partner having arousal problems? (After checking the sexual expression at the beginning of a relationship, this aspect should continue to be checked yearly.)
- In what ways are affection, intimacy, and sex different for each of you?

SII

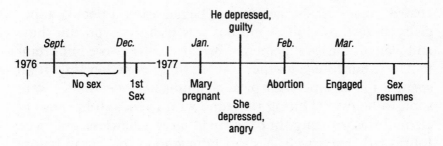

Case History

A conspiracy of silence had developed between John and Mary concerning the abortion. The event was never talked about, and neither of their families were told. The blowup over the abortion and the reconciliation that ensued seemed to signal the way situations were to be handled and solved. The loss of sexuality after the abortion until after the engagement gave both John and Mary time to think through what they wanted from each other. Both of their families approved of their relationship; however, the religious issue seemed to be a problem for John's mother. When Mary indicated a desire to become Catholic, John's mother and family were pleased. Mary's family did not interfere.

When the sudden engagement was announced, both families wondered if Mary was pregnant. "If so, better to wait," her family cautioned her. John's father, who had suffered a massive heart attack two weeks before, gave them his blessing and prayed he could live to be at the wedding. Both John and Mary felt "strangely secure" in their decision to marry. Despite some warnings from friends of Mary's regarding John's "wandering eye," university friends talked of showers and bachelor parties.

John and Mary decided to move in together in June. They rented an apartment, where they intended to live following the wedding. The wedding was planned for the university chapel in August. Some arguing began around details, especially about how John's mother was trying to run the show and plan all the arrangements. Bridal showers were important to Mary, but John's mother wanted them done her way. John spent a lot of time with pals, claiming his "free days" were soon to be over. During this time with friends, John's use of alcohol was growing. But the wedding was flawless, and even John's father felt well. A short honeymoon to Hawaii before school began proved restful and uneventful, and both partners seemed happy.

Wedding Planning/Wedding Honeymoon Questions

- How did your families react to the engagement/wedding?
- Were there any problems in the wedding planning process?
- Did you have any concerns before the wedding about the other person?
- Did you feel ready to get married at that time?
- Why did you get married then and not later?
- Was there a honeymoon? How did it go? Were your expectations met?
- What were your expectations, hopes, dreams as you began marriage?

SII

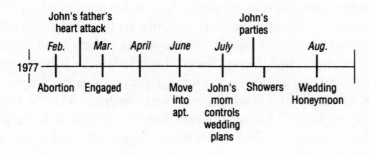

Case History

Coming back to the university and student life was a bit of a shock to the married couple. Mary assumed that they would be living a "normal" married life, sort of like her mom and dad. John, though, seemed to get caught up immediately in campus life and the old "frat system" he had been a part of. From when they first met, they had developed a few close friends who were also couples; however, one of these couples had since broken up, and the other had switched to another school. With the pressure of their junior year, working part-time jobs, and trying to save money by not eating out so much, John and Mary became homebodies. John became restless, and bouts of beer drinking, arguing, and depression seemed to follow. Mary kept her distance and felt he would outgrow being "trapped."

Sex was a source of both pleasure and tension. John would invite buddies and their girlfriends over for parties when Mary was working. The predictable tensions were in evidence when Mary would return home to the mess. Mary's interest in classical music and theater seemed to clash with John's tastes; often he would endure an opera or play if she would go out drinking with him and go to sports events. Mary's friend Monica reported during the fall that she had seen John with another woman. In late November, Mary told John she was pregnant.

Social Life Questions

- Did you socialize as individuals? (The couple's social life should be checked yearly.)
- Whose friends did you socialize with—his, hers, or both? What activities did you mesh into a new social network?
- Did you still hang on to previous systems to stay "unmarried"?

SII

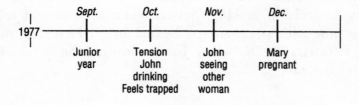

Case History

As John and Mary unfolded the experience of their attempts at creating an intimate relationship, a peculiar pattern seemed to develop. When John pushed for sexual contact, Mary withdrew. When sex occurred as a result of mutual desire, it seemed healthy but somehow contingent on subtle power plays. The association of sex with the possibility of pregnancy was a factor. Mary's growing distrust of John's secretive behavior, however, was a wedge between them. Blowups regarding trust were increasingly more frequent. Pregnancies seemed to follow bouts of insecurity and became dramatic points of decision making. Sexual behavior rose and fell in connection with pregnancies. Sexual intercourse continued until February 1978, when John admitted he was seeing another woman.

Sexuality Questions

- How did you perceive your sexual interaction?
- Any changes/arousal problems? (The sexual relationship should be checked each year.)
- How did each view their sexual changes?
- When did changes occur? (Is there a power struggle around sex?)

SII

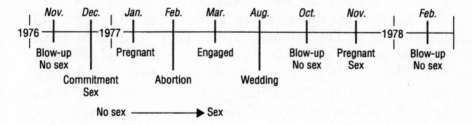

Case History

Mary's pregnancy in November 1977 was greeted with mixed feelings. Abortion was considered, but quietly dismissed. John blamed Mary for getting pregnant on purpose; she denied this and blamed his "constant need" for sex. Both sets of in-laws rallied about them and offered financial and emotional support. Considering that John and Mary were still another year from graduation, the future looked tough. With another blowup over John's "dating behavior" in February 1978, a truce seemed in order. Even without sexual intercourse with Mary (because the pregnancy was difficult), they settled down to school and married lie.

After the premature birth of John, Jr., in July, both parents "lived" for the child. With the death of their son (of SIDS) two months later, they were devastated. In spite of their grief, they got through the next year, graduated from college, and found jobs in Des Moines, Iowa. They seemed to grow together because of the death, but they were scared of having more children. In 1981, after marriage therapy, they decided to have a child. In 1982, Patrick was born, followed by Mark in 1986 and Lisa in 1991. All three children are healthy and wanted. Both Mary and John have continued to work, using day care and relatives to help with the children. John is a good father when he is there; however, he travels a great deal. Mary is "stuck" with the work, but thinks life is all right. Sex continues to be an issue, especially during and after pregnancies.

Pregnancies/Children/Parenting
Questions

- How was it decided to have children (mutual or un-planned)?
- Were there any changes after the birth of each child?
- What were the parenting responsibilities? How were they arranged?
- Did each of you have concerns regarding parenting? Is one too easy or the other too hard?
- Do you argue about parenting? Are you a team?

SII

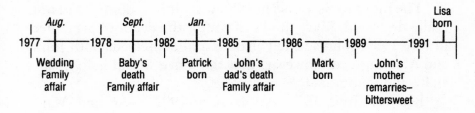

Case History

Both John and Mary have been intentional about carving out professional careers. The interruptions of a wedding, a child's death, pregnancies, and subsequent professional moves have not deterred them from full employment. Mary works as an office manager, which allows her to transfer her skills to various places of employment. She prefers to stay in one place and liked living in Des Moines and the house they had purchased. John's position as a manufacturer's representative is exciting and allows him to travel. Though he claims that he likes being home and being a father, he is gone an average of three to four days per week.

Finances are not an issue with this couple. Lack of quality time spent together is irritating, however, especially for Mary. She is a good manager, taking care of the domestic chores, but often is exhausted when John is ready to "reclaim" his territory at home.

The move to St. Louis in 1986 was "John's doing" and not really discussed. Mary thinks that after the death of his father in July 1985, John seemed anxious and depressed. Both John and Mary agreed, however, that the move would help financially and emotionally.

Between June 1986 and January 1992, John and Mary moved twice within the St. Louis area. In 1989, John's mother and her new husband moved to St. Louis. Although Mary and the children like John's mother, John is angry at his mother for remarrying. John's drinking again has become a concern for Mary.

Employment/Education/Financial Questions

- If one of you is not employed outside the home, how was that decided?
- Do work hours/schedules cause conflicts?
- Do volunteer service times/schedules cause conflicts?
- Are there arguments over work?
- Has a work/business/employment crisis caused abnormal stress on the couple? (Is the couple's relationship OK until faced with a significant life stressor?)
- Check career development of each person each year.
- How did they decide to handle their finances? (Whose family-of-origin blueprint was followed?)
- Are there problems in this arrangement?
- Is there any financial crisis (such as job loss, layoff, or business failure)? What is its effect on the relationship?

SII

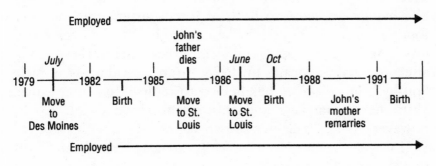

Case History

Since moving into an apartment together in the spring of 1977, John and Mary have moved a total of four times: to Des Moines in July 1979, to St. Louis in June 1986, and to new homes in St. Louis in August 1987 and October 1990. From John's perspective, the moves have been necessary to "house a growing family," but Mary believes they were because of John's restlessness.

Case History

Mary likes John's family and finds them exciting to be with. She has grown close to both of John's sisters and was very fond of his father. When the latter died in 1985, she felt a real loss. She believes both families have been helpful, especially after the baby's death in 1978. John's mother is a little "pushy", but distance has helped to temper this annoyance. With her remarriage and subsequent move to St. Louis, however, Mary "feels her presence."

John has never gotten too close to Mary's family and feels that they tend to judge him. John was very close to his father and misses him. His anger toward his own mother seems related to her remarriage and subsequent move to St. Louis.

Residence Changes/Moves Questions

- Are you renting a house?
- How was the decision made to buy a house(s)?
- How was the location decided?
- Were there any regrets regarding these decisions? (Check the decision-making process each time a move is made.)

SII

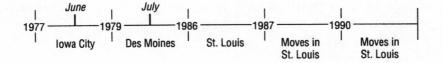

In-Laws Questions

- Is one person more involved with his or her family than the other?
- Are there any changes as a result of family-of-origin crises (such as death, divorce, illnesses, or financial problems)?
- Do the in-laws interfere? How? What is done about it? (Check throughout, especially in crisis periods.)

SII

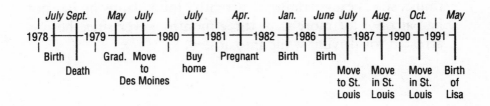

Case History

Throughout their relationship, John and Mary have noticed their different styles of expressing anger. John blows up and lets his anger go; often, it is directed back at Mary when she accuses him of affairs and drinking too much. Mary has a tendency to stuff her anger in silence, but when she feels there is proof of John's bad behavior, she tends to explode. As noted earlier, sex is usually the arena where the lasting effects of these conflicts are played out. Exhaustion and a conspiracy of silence wear them down over time, and they make up. Often John will say he is sorry, and Mary will quickly add that it is not all his fault.

Case History

The growing concern regarding John's substance abuse (alcohol) had been apparent for some years. In the courtship, John's excessive drinking was a worry for Mary. It seemed to accompany John's involvement with other women; also, when he was depressed, he tended to drink more. Mary had asked her physician about this and was referred to Al-Anon. Mary has also brought it up to counselors over the years, but John thinks she is exaggerating. Currently, John claims he has not had alcohol for more than three months—ever since he was arrested for driving while intoxicated.

Anger Questions

- Is anger expressed directly? Verbally? Behaviorally?
- Is anger expressed through attacking? Through withdrawal?
- How do you know when your partner is angry?
- Who wins? Who makes up?
- How often do you have conflicts? (Check throughout for changes.)
- Over what issues do you have conflict? (Do not get too bogged down in content.)
- Does conflict create distance, or does it maintain closeness?
- Are you afraid to fight? Afraid of closeness?

SII

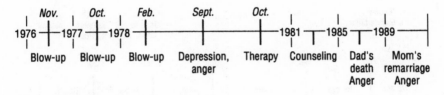

Substance Abuse Questions

- Monitor any development of increased, problematic, or abusive use of alcohol, drugs, or food.
- Is this a distancing mechanism? Is it an expression of anger?
- Also check for compulsive exercising or jogging, as these also can be distancing mechanisms.

SII

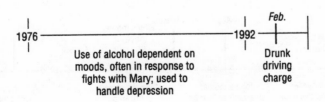

Table 5-1
Complete SII: Courtship to Present

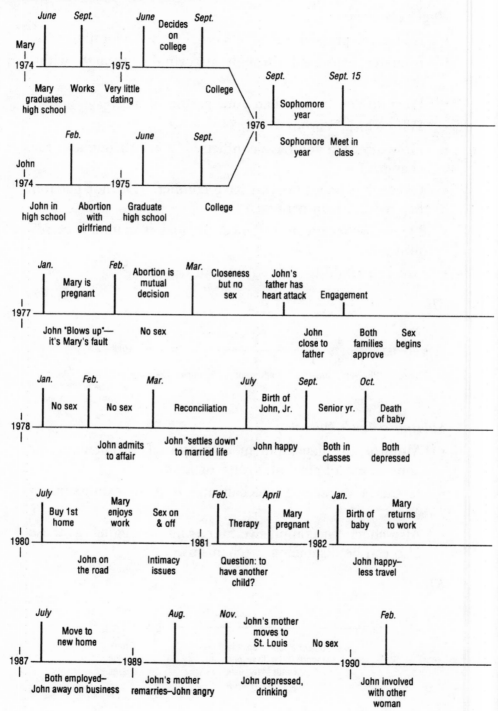

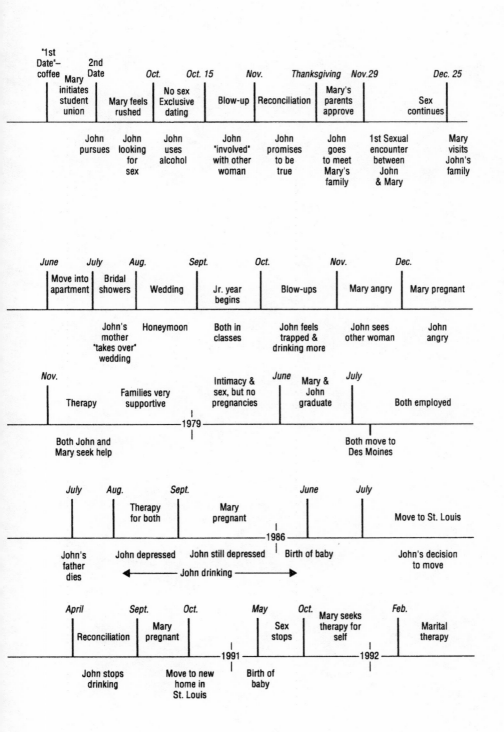

"1st Date"– coffee
Mary initiates student union

2nd Date

Oct.

Oct. 15
No sex Exclusive dating

Nov.
Blow-up

Thanksgiving
Reconciliation

Nov.29
Mary's parents approve

Dec. 25
Sex continues

Mary feels rushed

John pursues

John looking for sex

John uses alcohol

John "involved" with other woman

John promises to be true

John goes to meet Mary's family

1st Sexual encounter between John & Mary

Mary visits John's family

June
Move into apartment

July
Bridal showers

Aug.
Wedding

Sept.
Jr. year begins

Oct.
Blow-ups

Nov.
Mary angry

Dec.
Mary pregnant

John's mother "takes over" wedding

Honeymoon

Both in classes

John feels trapped & drinking more

John sees other woman

John angry

Nov.
Therapy

Families very supportive

Intimacy & sex, but no pregnancies

June
Mary & John graduate

July
Both employed

1979

Both John and Mary seek help

Both move to Des Moines

July

Aug.
Therapy for both

Sept.
Mary pregnant

June

July
Move to St. Louis

1986

John's father dies

John depressed

John still depressed
◄——— John drinking ———►

Birth of baby

John's decision to move

April
Reconciliation

Sept.
Mary pregnant

Oct.

May
Sex stops

Oct.
Mary seeks therapy for self

Feb.
Marital therapy

1991

1992

John stops drinking

Move to new home in St. Louis

Birth of baby

6

Searching Out a Direction:
Concluding the SII

You have been following along, watching the system emerge between John and Mary as we went through the SII. Rather than begin this chapter with theoretical considerations for doing the wrap-up of an SII, we will present the wrap-up we did for John and Mary. After looking at this we will discuss the rationale behind wrap-ups, provide comments on constructing them, and finally, note some directions regarding future therapy.

We have selected only one major theme to present in the wrap-up. Others might select one or more different themes to present. Each therapist will perceive the content differently and must respond to the perceived major themes. We believe it is important, however, not to present more than two or three themes in a wrap-up.

The wrap-up is presented with John and Mary looking at a simplified version of the SII on the board or newsprint. The therapist places the entire SII on the board prior to the session, highlighting those events from the history of the relationship that he or she wants to address. The SII used for this wrap-up is shown in simplified form, in Table 6–1.

As can be seen in the table, all of the events we have cited relate to the themes of bonding and triangulations. John

Table 6-1

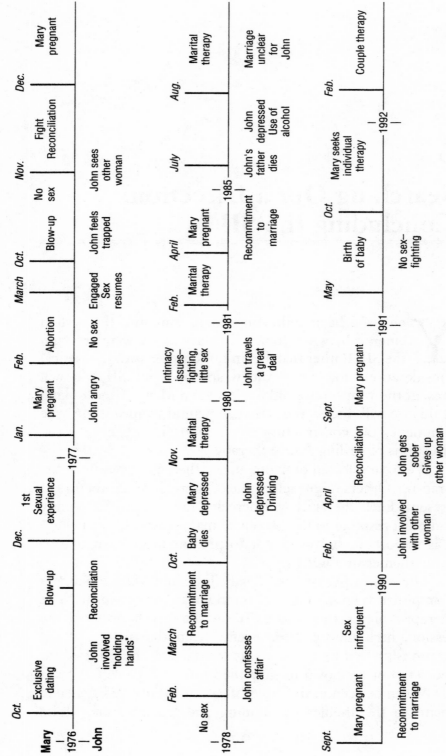

holding hands with another girl after he and Mary had decided to go steady is the first significant interactional dynamic in this relationship. It seems to set the tone for the entire relationship. It is an example of how either John or Mary responds to any attempt to heat up the relationship by cooling it down. Frequently, they make use of affairs or triangulations to cool down the relationship.

In presenting the wrap-up to John and Mary, we went through each of the significant events in Table 6–1, refreshed their memory as to those particular events, and indicated that these formed clues to our ideas about this relationship and the pattern that was emerging. After going through all of the clues with John and Mary listening and observing, we then went back and reviewed each of the significant events and indicated how each one of them signified the struggles the couple were having with intimacy and bonding.

We then highlighted what we saw as an emerging pattern. To us, what is important in exploring this or any pattern is to try to help the couple figure out what appears to be a recurring dynamic that creates a dysfunctional pattern of communication in their particular system. In reviewing the attaching-detaching pattern discussed in Chapter 3, we paid particular attention to a couple who have created for themselves a recurring problem that draws them into the experience of intimacy, but creates behavioral difficulties in maintaining that intimacy. There are several aspects of this relationship that we think provide excellent clues to this pattern's existence. After completing the SII with the couple, we felt these dynamics were rather easy to spot.

Table 6–1 shows dramatic incidents in the history of this marriage that might reflect this particular dynamic. Often during the early dating experiences, one or the other partner in an attaching-detaching relationship might appear very much interested in pursuing the other person, even to the extent of violating appropriate boundaries. Often the response of the person who is being pursued is to create rather rigid boundaries or to go silent. Many times, the dynamic appears almost in stereotypical format, where one of the individuals is very active, while the other individual is very secretive. Also, the attaching personality is not only more active in attempting to cement the relationship but, when feeling blocked, finds himself or herself becoming angry and withdrawing from the pursuit. It is usually when this absence of pursuit is experienced by the detached member of the relationship that he or she begins to reverse the dynamic and to pursue the other individual.

After presenting the emerging pattern in the SII, John and Mary were given some time to ask any questions needed to clarify our ideas, and then they were sent home to think about the wrap-up and return the following week. When John and Mary returned, they indicated that their struggle over intimacy was indeed a centerpiece of their relationship. We went over the wrap-up again briefly, fitting into it other details provided by John and Mary that had not come out earlier. Both John and Mary thought that their conflict over intimacy was a dynamic that was present in their parents' marriages. Following a brief discussion of the intimacy struggles in the separate families of origin, a new contract was made to spend three sessions exploring this particular pattern to determine to what degree they had either replicated the parental marriages or were delegated to do so by triangulation.

We have indicated that we were most struck by the bonding and triangulation issues in John and Mary's relationship history. Other therapists might look at expressions of anger within the relationship, others might see self-esteem issues as the dominant theme, and still others might be struck by the dependency issues in the relationship. This marriage, like all relationships, has multiple themes. The task for the therapist is to decide which themes are most important and which would be of most benefit in developing some kind of therapeutic change in the couple's relationship.

Developing a Wrap-Up

Sometimes comments and observations are made at each session as the evaluation proceeds; however, major themes and patterns are held until the wrap-up. To us, the wrap-up means helping the couple get some sense of what the therapist sees and experiences about their relationship. It may be a description of how the therapist experiences the intimacy or distance in the marriage; how each partner tends to build up his or her own low self-esteem by robbing from the other; the anger, pain, and dependency that are experienced but cannot be talked about; or the struggle for power that takes place in the relationship. What the therapist describes in the wrap-up is designed to give the couple some sense of how they behave, of their system or interactional pattern.

The choice is always there as to whether the therapist wants to work with this particular couple and whether they are ready for work. By contracting to evaluate a relationship (by completing the SII), the therapist and the couple have a natural opportunity to end the process. Some couples find that just in completing the SII they have achieved sufficient awareness into their relationship and the changes they would like to make. Other couples, having completed the SII, see this as an opportunity to contract for further therapy.

Administrative Issues

When we do a SII, we try to structure the sessions in such a way that we end up concluding the SII time line at the beginning of the wrap-up session. This may mean slowing down the SII exploration in the previous session so that you have the last six to twelve months of the relationship history to complete before beginning with the wrap-up.

As the therapist is gathering information, exploring themes, and obtaining a picture of the relationship, it is important to be able to view the relationship rhythm and personality as a whole. Being able to identify major or recurring themes leads to accurate analysis, metaphors, analogies, or reframings of the relationship. An accurate assessment is critical to identifying tasks for change.

Foundational Themes for the Wrap-Up

If any of the following basic and foundational themes appear in the SII, they need to be considered for inclusion in the wrap-up. As you will note, they are not mutually exclusive.

1. *Fusion/symbiosis:* How stuck together are the partners? Does each seem overly dependent, asking the other to be the main source of happiness? How do they tolerate differences in thoughts, feelings, and behavior? Is all their energy going into the relationship or into trying to change the other person? What do they leave for themselves?

2. *Expression of anger:* Do they deny or repress anger? Is it shoved underground? Are they attacking? Are they pseudohostile (fighting to stay close)? Do they make love by fighting, or do they fight to get distance? Do they think that love and commitment rule out fighting?

3. *Power:* Are there constant power struggles occurring over sex, distance, or personal habits? How does each person exhibit his or her power? Is one covertly powerful and one overtly powerful?

4. *Self-esteem:* Does either have unrealistically high expectations? Does either expect the worst? Is one robbing the other to feel good? Is the other being robbed to look good or validate himself or herself? Do they have great difficulty asking for what they want? Expressing anger? Are they overly sensitive to conflict and thus avoid it? Or do they attack so that they will not get attacked or have to express their vulnerability? Does either have elaborate dreams that do not match reality and thus create pain?

5. *Bonding/commitment:* How connected are they? If they do not fight and do not have sex, then there probably is a distance or commitment issue. How committed are they? Are decisions made bilaterally, or are they made unilaterally without consultation? Have they really decided to be married, or are they "playing house?"

6. *Blueprint/family-of-origin struggles:* Does the couple seem to be involved in a chronic struggle over whose family blueprint to follow? Is there a social class struggle? A religious struggle? Are there racial/cultural struggles?

7. *Affairs/triangulation:* Are there, or were there, any romantic affairs? Were they efforts to heat up the relationship, or to maintain distance? Are children triangulated to maintain distance? Does the relationship need a third party? Are hobbies, activities, work, friends used as "affairs?"

8. *Dependency:* Does one partner allow abnormal domination and control by the other? Does the other want abnormal control? Is one partner overly dependent on the other for making decisions? Does the other partner need to be depended upon to make these decisions? Was there a rapid, short courtship? A quick move to sex? Does either blame their unhappiness on the other? Are they easily devastated when their partner gets angry?

9. *Recurring patterns of interactions:* Do their particular styles of interaction reflect problems with intimacy and distancing behaviors? Do themes of dependency seem evident in how the couple interact? When and how do certain behavior patterns recur? Do certain behavior styles of interaction ensure no change in the presenting problem?

More Comments on Developing a Wrap-Up

Developing a wrap-up of a relationship from the diagnostic elements for the couple can be a blending of the creative/artistic and deductive/scientific talents of the therapist. Succinct analogies, metaphors, and reframing can be developed.

The most important element in developing the wrap-up is to present the couple with an analysis that is different from their own analysis of the relationship. In the SII process, the couple has handed you the relationship and its parts as they see it; in order to create the opportunity for change, the therapist must hand it back to them in a way that is less familiar.

Second, the wrap-up must be bilateral. The best reframing includes all of the major aspects of the couple's interactional system and how both parties were involved in creating the system, either actively or passively.

Third, be sure to use illustrations from the SII to build your case. If you are concerned about the distancing of a couple, for example, illustrate your idea based on the many separations they had. A farm family we were working with lived on the homestead farm in a mobile home alongside of the parents' house. The husband was at his father's beck and call. Even though he was forty-eight years old, it was as if he was eighteen; he was more married to his father and farm than to his wife. The observation was used in the wrap-up with profound, growth-producing results.

Fourth, be conscious of developing a wrap-up that is at the couple's level of seeing the world. Use metaphors with couples who are not highly cognitive, for example, who would not benefit from a highly intellectualized analysis of the couple system.

Lastly and obviously, it is important to match the theme of the wrap-up to the couple. If the wrap-up and accompanying reframing are too far off base, they will fall flat with the couple.

The Need for Further Therapy

Following completion of the wrap-up, a decision needs to be made regarding the possibility of further therapy. Four basic possibilities exist: no further therapy needed; therapy on specific issues; work on separation from family of origin, and therapy halted.

The Joy of Having a Map: No Further Therapy Needed

There are some couples who need no further therapy. To therapists who have not used the SII before, the idea that it could produce growth in and of itself seems unbelievable. The fact that some couples neither desire nor need more therapy seems to rest on two basic dynamics. First, as Carl Whitaker has been fond of saying for years, there are some couples who enter therapy not to change what goes on in their relationship, but rather to understand it. They can not figure out where they are and what is happening; they can not "see" their map. The SII helps couples see what is going on their relationship and to put disjointed pieces together.

Second, the SII can have a powerful therapeutic impact when it is infused with dyadic questioning. The dyadic questioning style forces the couple to view their own system from the outside. Thus the couple is constantly learning, often for the first time, what each other's perceptions are about all of the nodal events and aspects of the relationship. In addition, the dyadic questioning style is particularly helpful in dealing with couples who have difficulty expressing their thoughts and feelings directly. In all cases, however, dyadic questioning exposes the couple to a new way of experiencing itself. This experience can be so powerful (and the map can become so clear) that the couple has virtually completed therapy when the SII is finished.

A New Map and Guide: Therapy on Specific Issues

If the couple would like to continue work for change after the wrap-up is presented, a new contract can be developed. If the therapist feels that he or she does not have the skill to address the specific change issues a couple desires, he or she should refer them and offer to share the evaluation with the other therapist. Usually, however, if an accurate assessment (wrap-up) has been presented to the couple and the latter wish to work on change, tasks and assignments can be developed directly from the assessment. Finding out what the problem is should logically lead to steps for change; identifying steps can even be done with the couple's assistance in the sessions. The Appendix to this volume also lists books on topics frequently identified as being areas of further work (such as communication, depression, roles, parenting, or sex therapy). Often some change has already taken place from the SII process itself, particularly if the therapist has used dyadic questioning.

Searching for the Hidden Maps: Work on Separation from Family of Origin

It has been well established in family theory (and family therapy theory) that the degree of separation a person has from his or her family of origin can be an important indicator of marital success. The degree to which a person is able to move in status from child to adult, to become a peer with his or her parents, and to abandon any parental dysfunctional patterns has something to do with the ability of that individual to succeed in marriage. Often when we have finished presenting a warp-up to a couple, they frequently remark, "How come we behave this way?" or "Where did we ever learn to relate in this fashion?" The answer we most frequently give is as follows: "Probably from your parents. They were your first models, and whatever problems they didn't get settled in their marriages were passed on down to you." At this point, we most commonly propose a new contract: to evaluate each partner's family of origin and search for the maps these two individuals are using, unaware that they are being guided by instructions from the previous generations.

Research

Since the early 1950s, significant research has been done on the importance of individuals' ability to separate psychologically from their families of origin. The people who adapt to couple life best in America seem to have two characteristics. First, they are individuals who have been able to leave home, psychologically speaking, in that they no longer ask their parents to take responsibility for their lives; in short, the child has become an adult. Second, they also have had an opportunity to live alone after leaving home and before entering marriage. Living alone and being able to survive (both emotionally and financially) are important in that people must have an opportunity to establish their own psychological identity. These two themes are recounted numerous times in the literature on family theory and family therapy.

Individuals who have not left home emotionally and psychologically experience greater difficulties in life in a number of ways. First, they keep getting tangled up in family problems. Their own marital relationships are chronically in crisis because of the crises that are going on in the larger family. Struggles between the mother and father, between the parents and one or more of the children, or between adult children interfere with and cause friction in the marriage.

Second, people who have not left home psychologically tend to look for spouses who will continue the parenting of the biological parents. Because families who hang onto their children prevent their children from growing up psychologically, these individuals look for a spouse not in terms of a peer—a fellow adult with whom they can establish an intimate relationship—but in terms of another person who will take care of them. That kind of relationship, however, is frequently beset with problems, because chances are that the other spouse is looking for the very same kind of partner. Thus, two people who are both looking for a parent depend on each other to be the good, kind, and patient parent who will enable them to be a child forever.

Third, these people tend to have more physical and somatic problems than others. The research on psychosomatic illness documents the fact that people who are still emotionally tied to their families of origin as adults are physically sick more frequently than those who are more independent.

Fourth, people who have not psychologically separated from their parents usually come from homes in which the parents do not want them to do so. They have been encouraged not to grow up, not to take charge of their own lives—in short, to remain children. With this attitude in the family of origin, the individual will have difficulty functioning as an adult.

Conducting Family-of-Origin Work

Thus, the purpose of our second contract, the family-of-origin exploration (FOE), is to take a look at the degree of separation that exists between each of the persons and his or her family of origin. The FOE is designed to help the couple assess whether they have an excessive attachment to their parents and whether they take responsibility for their own lives, as well as to give them some sense of their need for growth regarding their family of origin.

Parents as Models. There is no doubt that parents are the first human beings that we, as children, come to know. Our father is the first male we come to know, our mother is the first female we come to know, and our parents are also the first husband-wife team we come to know. Thus, couple expectations, attitudes, and behavior patterns are not born into us; we learn them from our parents. Children who have only one parent, or whose parents are absent or deficient in some way, often creatively find substitutes (such as grandparents, aunts, uncles, neighbors, and teachers). Research clearly supports the idea that parents are powerful models. Naturally, some models are better than others; thus, parents in an indirect fashion either help or hinder couples in establishing and maintaining married life.

Families in which conflict exists in the parental marriage tend to have children who take one of two courses. On the one hand, some of the children will repeat the pattern of the parental marriage. It is almost as if these children, seeing their parents struggling with problems they cannot resolve, need to duplicate those problems and to solve them for both themselves and their parents. Thus, many couples will almost identically replicate the problems or patterns of their parents' marriages, using the same maps. On the other hand, there are some people who try to prevent repeating the conflicts of their parents' marriages by behaving in exactly opposite ways. Sometimes this works, and other times it only creates the opposite problems.

There seems to be a particular kind of pain experienced by people who, as they were growing up, perceived their same-sex parent as losing in the marital relationship. Although marriages are usually well balanced, with husbands and wives either both losing or both winning, children often do not perceive it that way. If the same-sex parent was perceived as losing, the adult child may be difficult to live with because he or she does not want to duplicate that parent's defeat. In like manner, the adult child who saw the same-sex parent winning may seek to dominate or get his or her own way.

In the FOE, our purpose is to look at and trace not only the parental models that a man and woman bring into their relationship, but also how these models influence the partner's behavior with each other. Again, our purpose has to do with heightening the couple's awareness of the models.

Format for the Exploration. We place the family-of-origin exploration after the SII. There are several reasons why this work is not placed first or included in the SII. First, the therapist frequently does not know one or both parties, and placing the SII first allows the therapist a chance to become acquainted with the couple. Second, people seem to find it easier to talk about themselves and their dating and marital or cohabiting experience than about their families of origin. Since most couples have experienced their dating relationship as pleasant and had a state of heightened awareness about their relationship as they moved to the wedding, this seems to be an easier starting place for them.

It is important for the therapist to explain the reasons for the FOE as clearly and as fully as possible. The issue of the impact of parental modeling should be stressed. Some families will, upon reflection, see the usefulness of the FOE; others will remain resistant. If a person or couple is resistant, it is best to respect their feelings. Sometimes focusing on the reason for these feelings will overcome the resistance. The FOE can also be conducted with the willing partner and focus on both families, although this is more difficult. When only one partner is present, however, it is important for the therapist to focus on what the absent partner might say if he or she were present, thereby making that person a "present" as possible. The use of predictions is useful for the person's reflection on and consideration of the implications of the partner's behavior. We suggest at least three sessions as the basic format: one session can be devoted to each family, and a third session can be spent in the wrap-up. Often two sessions are spent on each partner's family of origin, and a fifth on the wrap-up and integration of the two families of origin.

The process of looking at each person's family of origin involves an examination of all the interactions and levels of functioning the family. In most counseling cases, this will not be difficult to accomplish unless the family has many children in it or many marriages, divorces, and other events make it exceedingly complex to comprehend. We divide the FOE into seven section: (1) the siblings as individuals, (2) sibling interactions, (3) parent-child interactions, (4) husband-wife interactions, (5) family interactional style, (6) parental models, and (7) wrap-up. As in the SII, we have found that a visual aid is important in effectively dealing with this material. We

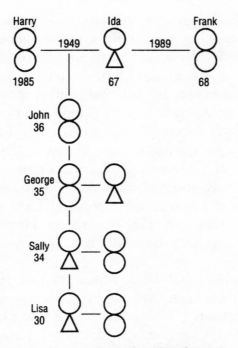

Figure 6–1: John's Family of Origin

suggest either a white-board or newsprint. Because the therapist will want to keep the diagram for future reference, the use of newsprint or a notepad will save the task of copying the information form from the whiteboard.

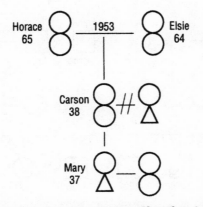

Figure 6–2: Mary's Family of Origin

The methodology for the family-of-origin exploration begins with drawing the family as a two-generation genogram. Our basic format is shown in Figures 6–1 and 6–2, which illustrate John and Mary's separate families. From Figure 6–1, the reader can see that John is thirty-six years of age and has one younger brother (George, who is thirty five) and two younger sisters (Sally, who is thirty-four, and Lisa, who is thirty). John's parents are Harry, who died in 1985, and Ida, age sixty-seven. Ida married Frank, who is sixty-eight, in 1989. Figure 6–2 shows that Mary is thirty-seven years of age and has one older brother (Carson, age thirty-seven), who is divorced. Her parents are Horace, age sixty-five, and Elsie, age sixty-four; they have been married for forty years.

Recently there has been much interest in the use of genograms in marriage and family therapy, with the result that the format has been standardized. As we use the genogram in the FOE, we use both the two-generational figure-type diagrams shown in Figures 6–1 and 6–2 and the standardized format shown in figure 6–3. We have found that the figure-type diagramming can greatly personalize the FOE process by adding faces or similar attributes when discussing and drawing the couple, their families of origin and their interactions or quality of their connectedness. Thought, creativity, and humor seem to flow from use of the personal-

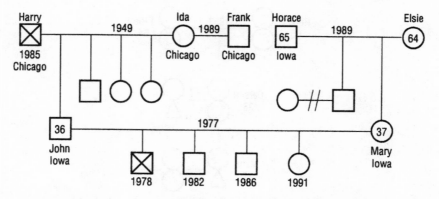

Figure 6–3: Standardized Genogram of John and Mary

ized figures in comparison to the sole use of the square-and-circle format. We do use the standardized symbols as we expand the chart to include the details of three or four generations.

Figure 6–3 shows John and Mary in their families of origin using the symbols and notations that have become standardized in genograms. The information shows the couple, John and Mary, and family information back through their parents. The genogram also shows the birth order positions of each family member and the gender of siblings. John is the oldest of our children; Mary is the younger of two children. What might be the implications of their birth orders for their relationship? We believe that an understanding of family constellation and birth order can be useful to the therapist, not for predictive purposes but for understanding interpersonal dynamics and behavior. The therapist will benefit from reading further about the use of sibling position in marital relationships and interpreting genograms using family constellation information.

As we use the genogram, our goal is to obtain both interactional and historical information. Also, demographic information should be obtained and can add to knowledge and insight gained by the couple and therapist. Specifically, such things as age, place of birth, place of current residence, schooling/training completed, and current occupation are basic. In Figure 6–3, we see that Mary, her parents, and brother are all living in Iowa. John also lives in Iowa, where he met Mary; notice that John's family, however, lives in Chicago.

The style of the family-of-origin exploration is similar to that of the SII. Again, this style makes use of many questions designed to expand the thinking process of the couple. It is important to keep the sessions moving and flowing. Although the therapist needs to take enough time to get the flavor of each of the persons and their interactions with other members of the family, it is necessary not to become bogged down in too many details.

The goal, at the end, is to present the couple with a wrap-up that will give them some new way of understanding their families of origin. Family-of-origin work and genogram usage are not simply about collecting historical facts: they gather data in a way that makes a difference (through the use of dyadic questioning) and reframe it in a way that also makes a difference.

Siblings as Individuals. We begin the FOE by finding out the names of each of the children in the family, their ages, and where each is living. We are also interested in knowing how each child is faring in terms of his or her success in life. This includes the marital functioning of the siblings, if they are married; if any of the siblings have experienced a divorce, we wish to have the person characterize his or her understanding of the reason for the nature of the marital conflict and the subsequent divorce. We are interested in characterization of her/his brothers and sisters not only by their success in life, but also by their personalities and temperaments. Are they outgoing or shy, talkative or quiet, easily angered or even-tempered, assertive or passive, opinionated or agreeable?

The issue in this particular segment is the separation of siblings from the family of origin. Generally speaking, the children who are functioning the best in adulthood and are succeeding in marital life are going to be those who have been able to establish some sense of separateness from the family of origin. Sometimes we can pick this up on geography; the children who are within shouting distance of parents or who have gone to the farthest part of the earth are often the children who have had or are having the most difficulty with parents and leaving home. The purpose of this section, then, is to get an idea of the degree to which other members of this family have been able to leave home psychologically.

Sibling Interactions. In this particular segment, we are primarily interested in the manner in which the children in the family got along with each other in their childhood. Our process is one of dyad testing: we take the oldest child and look at his or her relationship to the second oldest child, the third oldest child, and so on. Then we take the second oldest child and look at his or her relationships to the other children. We use all the dyad combinations of each child and his or her relationship to every other child until the entire sibling system is explored.

The issue in our study of these dyads has to do with the manner in which these individuals related to each other in the growing-up process and whether any of the children in the family functioned in a substitute-parent role. It is possible for a person to have been raised in such a way that he or she developed a close primary relationship with an older child, separating from whom poses as many problems as does leaving the relationship with parents. It is also possible that the child who has functioned as a substitute parent will have difficulty in moving into a relationship in which he or she cannot continue to function in a caretaking role.

We are also concerned about the spacing of the children. If there is too much space between children, the possibility of a sense of isolation exists. If more than five years separates two children, for example, it is likely that one or both might have experienced life as an only child does. In contrast, if children are closely spaced and if there are many of them, the possibility of feelings of inattention exists.

Parent-Child Interactions. The purpose of this section is to examine the nature and the characteristics of the intergenerational dyads: each parent and each child in the family. How did they get along? How did they express anger toward each other? How did they express affection toward each other? Who won when they fought? How were they similar or dissimilar from each other?

In addition to exploring the kind of interactions each parent had with each child, we are particularly interested in each person's perception of the preference order of parents in dealing with children. In other words, we are interested in knowing from John whom he thinks his father liked best and why, and whom his mother liked best and why. If John's partner has been around the family enough to comment on this issue, we also ask for *her* perception of these answers. It is also valuable to ask about who each parent liked least and why; again, double-check the perception with the partner's opinion, if possible.

The issue in this section is an examination of the role of favorites in the family. People who are the first choice of a parent often have stronger attachments to that parent. Sometimes parents attach their ambitions and dreams to the favorite child and try to live vicariously through him or her. Favorite children may, in fact, find it more difficult to leave home or to have the parent allow them to leave home.

One should not overlook, however, the role of negative attachment. The child who feels that he or she is never good enough has a kind of attachment to parents, just as does the child who never does wrong. Again, the issue of attachments has something to do with the psychological freedom of the adult child.

Husband-Wife Interactions. In this section, we are particularly interested in the nature of the parent marital dyad. Our interest in this is very similar to our interest in the relationship of the presenting couple. We wonder about power: who was in charge of the marriage, how did they handle decision making, and how was the power balanced. How did the child know when one parent was angry with the other? When they argued, who got hurt, and who initiated peace overtures? If they did not argue, how did they demonstrate their disagreement? Where did it come out, and how far underground was it? How did each child know when one parent was pleased with what the other said and did? How comfortable were the parents with affection? Could they both give it and receive it? How did each child perceive the level of self-esteem in each parent? If low self-esteem was present, how did this affect the relationship? Was either parent oversensitive? Was either vulnerable? How, then, did he or she handle pain?

One of the issues in this section is the nature of the parents' marriage in regard to these dynamics. How parents handled anger, affection, self-esteem, dependency, closeness, and many other issues will provide a model that has an impact on adult children in many and subtle ways. Another issue has to do with the nature of the parental marriage. If the coalition between the mother and father is firm and healthy, they will be able to let their children grow up and establish their own lives. If, however, the marital relationship has turned bitter or sour, then one or both parents will frequently attempt to attach themselves to one of the children to make up for what is not happening in the marriage. If there is a psychological split in the parental marital relationship (whether it leads to a divorce or not), the possibility that one or more of the children will be chosen as a surrogate or substitute spouse is high.

Children who are chosen to fill the role of a spouse because of a bad marriage often have difficulty in leaving home. Psychologically, the parents in a crippled marriage will attempt to rescue some sense of hopefulness, happiness, and esteem from a child. It is difficult enough being married to one spouse, let alone two; when a parent chooses a child as a substitute mate, the child will have difficulty moving to and maintaining his or her own marriage unless he or she can divorce from the marriage with the parent.

Family Interactional Style. In this particular section, we are interested in two dynamics of the family of origin: family adaptability and family cohesion. Therapists interested in an instrument that assesses these two dynamics should consider using the Enrich inventory or FACES scales.

In regard to family adaptability, first, we explore the nature of leadership in the family of origin. Was it easy to identify the leaders in the family? Did the same person or persons exercise leadership roles during the duration of the child-raising years, or did different individuals act as leaders? Was it difficult to tell who was in charge of the family? Leadership roles are connected with family rules and how families either maintain their rules rigidly or have no rules at all. We also explore the nature of the family rules. Were rules constantly changing, or were they relatively fixed? Did different people carry out different tasks at different times, or were the same tasks maintained throughout the duration of the growing-up years? Was it clear who was to do what when, or were household responsibilities shifted around from person to person?

In both of these aspects (family leadership and family rules), we are interested in attempting to assess the nature of the family's adaptability. On one end of the continuum is a leadership style that is very fixed and unchanging, which usually results in rules that are rigidly maintained. At the other end is a leadership style that is constantly changing, which usually results in family rules that are very chaotic and constantly changing as well. In the middle of this spectrum is a leadership style that has some flexibility in it, with the result that the family rules also are stable but flexible.

In regard to family cohesion, we are also interested in two different aspects. First, we explore the degree to which the members of the family of origin were able to cooperate with each other. Could they ask each other for assistance? Did they consult each other in regard to family decisions? In some families, there is a great deal of cooperation, whereas in others, people tend to each take care of their own things and manage by themselves. Second, we explore the degree of togetherness with which the family operated. Did they spend their free time with each other? Did they generally do things together? Some families have a great deal of separateness in their activities, with members spending little free time with each other. Did the family feel close, or did members feel distant from each other?

In regard to both requesting assistance and togetherness, we are interested in exploring the continuum of family cohesion. Some families operate with very little cohesion and thus have members who tend to assist each other very little and to operate rather independently from each other; the cohesive style in these families may be described as disengaged. At the other end of the spectrum are families that do almost all things together and whose members assist each other very little and to operate rather independently from each other; the cohesive style in these families may be described as disengaged. At the other end of the spectrum are families that do almost all things together and whose members assist each other a great deal. These families have a cohesive style that could be described as enmeshed. In the middle of the continuum are families that can operate with both some togetherness and some separateness, thus having a cohesive style that combines independence and dependence.

The Wrap-Up. We have been attempting to outline a process for conducting the FOE. It is an orderly process, but one that is designed to establish how a family works and what makes it tick. We have attempted to provide the reader with some of the kinds of things we look for in our understanding of how families work. Although not all of this information is necessarily meant to be passed along to the couple, it does help explain some of our understandings of family life.

Each therapist will probably see a given family in a somewhat different way. Each much respond to what he or she sees, what impresses him or her, what touches or concerns him or her. Whatever is included in the wrap-up, however, the therapist must provide the couple with a new and different way of looking at and understanding their families of origin. This will help both partners to expand their thinking about the nature of human relationships and their own relationship.

We have attempted to provide the therapist with some theoretical background. Again, one of the important issues in determining whether a couple has a successful relationship is the nature of the parental marriage. When parental marriages do not function well, a psychological split develops between husband and wife. Even if they have not divorced, the presence of the split poses great problems for one or more of the children. When barriers develop in the relationship and bitterness sets in, the choosing by one or both partners of a child to become a substitute mate means that the child selected is going to develop a strong attachment to the parent. This may hinder, if not cripple, the adult child's ability to find a suitable mate and maintain that relationship. The healthy parental marriage and the parental marriage that is psychologically split are both models that have a powerful impact on the child's adult relationships.

In addition to describing the nature of the parental marriage to the couple, we also discuss the family interactional style in terms of family adaptability and family cohesion. Therapists who make use of the Enrich assessment instrument can insert the material from the inventory and those two dynamics at this point in time. After the therapist discusses the dynamics of adaptability and cohesion with the couple and notes where each of the families of origin fall on these continua, the data on the Enrich printout will give him or her a sense of the degree to which the two families of origin are either very similar or very different from each other. As we have said before, the greater the difference, the greater the likelihood of conflict; but even so, the difference can be seen as enriching and can be used to facilitate the growth of each person to learn something of the other's style.

When presenting the wrap-up on the family of origin to each person, we suggest that the discussion be addressed to the partner in dyadic questioning style. If one describes John's family of origin to him, for example, he will either defend the material or be preoccupied with relating to the therapist. But if one talks to Mary about John's family instead, John is able to listen and free his mind to absorb what is being said. If, after the description, the adult child of the family of origin just described wishes to comment on it, the therapist can then answer any questions. The primary focus is reporting the therapist's observations of the family of origin as determined from the information and data generated. Assuming that one is careful and accurate, there should be little rebuttal.

After completing the FOE wrap-up, the therapist can pull it together with the SII wrap-up and integrate them for the couple. With all the maps on the table, the couple can now address the issues identified by the two processes. As in the case of the SII, some couples will find the family-of-origin work therapeutic in and of itself and may need little further work. This is likely to occur when the following dynamics are present: The therapist has made use of family-of-origin homework (such as sending each partner back to interview parents, siblings, aunts, and uncles, or involving parents in some of the sessions); the couple has as their primary drive the goal to understand the maps and figure out how they all fit together; and the therapist has successfully unhooked some of the cross-generational collusions that had caused the part-ner(s) to remain triangulated in the parental marriage(s). Some couples, though, will need further work. If you have identified issues of low self-esteem in the family maps, for example, this issue can then be addressed in further therapy.

A New Map Without a Guide: Therapy Halted

After presentation of the wrap-up and identifying areas for change comes the consideration of the readiness of the couple to work on change. The timing of when the couple is ready to address their relationship issues is not to be ignored by the therapist. A couple may agree with an assessment, understand it, and cognitively want to address the issues—but not at the present time. Low pain level, unwillingness to risk, or the functionality of the dynamics may prevent significant move-ment with some couples. Possibly, the therapist should then take a distinct, resistance-based paradoxical mode, using a "stay the same," "this works for you in these ways," or "not ready" approach. In fact, the preceding injunctions should have been built into the wrap-up if those dynamics were picked up during the SII. In these situations, it is often best to take a break from therapy with the couple until they are ready to work. This is an inherent therapeutic paradox that might prompt them to draw a new relationship map for themselves. Ownership of the new and paradoxical map may prompt new directions that might very well prove to be the basis for a new therapeutic journey.

Conclusion

By now the reader may be wondering whether or not the couple has been inundated by the amount of material that has been evoked. We hope that this is so! By getting into the SII, the therapist can raise all kinds of issues, bringing up concerns that have never been verbalized and probably never even perceived. By doing so, he or she has the effect of shuffling the pain around, evening it up so that no one person stands out as "the problem" or as cleaner than the other.

We think that the SII also provides for a more total view of the human beings. By going through the experience of looking at their relationship, couples get a sense of how their own history is a unique blending of both pain and pleasure, that it is not in fact one big blob of pain.

The SII also allows couples to develop greater awareness about their mutual responsibilities for growth, interaction, and pain. In addition, it allows the therapist to participate in a special way, sharing his or her knowledge, creative imagination, and stirring responses. The nineteenth-century social analyst Walter Bagehut once commented in regard to royalty that "its mystery is its life. We dare not let daylight in upon the magic." We have come to believe, however, that the SII allows us to talk about the mysterious life and/or death of a relationship and are able to allow daylight in upon its magical aspects. If nothing else, the therapist and the couple have challenged the mystery of the relationship, have examined its health and dissatisfactions, and—without magic—are able to talk about "real therapy" and the possibility of continued movement and change. The real mystery and difficulty in couple therapy often revolves not around the couple's unwillingness to talk about their relationship, but around the therapist's inability to find a structure in which they can do so easily. It is our hope that the SII will preserve the beauty and the mystery of the relationship and at the same time introduce sufficient reality to dispel the myths and magic that might be preserving its pathology.

Appendix

The following books deal with specific topics that may become the focus of couple therapy following the SII. This list is purposefully not exhaustive. The reader is encouraged to integrate the process of the SII—and information gained form it—into the ongoing treatment of the couple, family, or individual.

Aging

Billig, N. 1993. *Growing older and wiser: Coping with expectations, challenges, and changes in the later years.* New York: Lexington.

Viorst, J. 1986. *Necessary losses.* New York: Simon & Schuster.

Wolinsky, M. 1991. *A heart of wisdom: Marital counseling with older and elderly couples.* New York Brunner/Mazel.

Communication and Decision Making

Thomas, E. J. 1977. *Marital communication and decision making.* New York: Free Press.

Stuart, R. B. 1980. *Helping couples change.* New York: Guilford.

Depression

Beach, S.R.H., Sandeen, E. E., and O'Leary, K. D. 1990. *Depression in marriage.* New York: Guilford.

Hinchliffe, M. K., Hooper, D., and Roberts, F. J. 1978. *The melancholy marriage.* New York: Wiley.

Divorce

Ahrons, C., and Rodgers, R., 1987. *Divorced families: A multidisciplinary developmental view.* New York: Norton.
Teyber, E. 1992. *Helping children cope with divorce.* New York: Lexington.

Extended Family

Carlin, V. F., and Greenberg, V. 1992. *Should Mom live with us?* New York: Lexington.
Framo, J. L. 1992. *Family-of-origin therapy.* New York: Brunner/Mazel.
McGoldrick, M., and Gerson, R. 1985. *Genograms in family assessment.* New York: Norton.

Finances

Poduska, B. E. 1992. *For love and money: A guide to finances and relationships.* Pacific Grove, CA: Brooks/Cole.

Parenting

Briggs, D. C. 1975. *Your child's self-esteem: The key to life.* Garden City, NY: Doubleday.
Cline, V. B. 1980. *How to make your child a winner.* New York: Walker.
Rosenberg, E. B. 1992. *The adoption lifecycle: The children and their families through the years.* New York: Free Press.
Satir, V. 1988. *The new peoplemaking.* Palo Alto, CA: Science and Behavior Books.

Premarriage and Remarriage

Stahmann, R. F., and Hiebert, W. J. 1987. *Premarital counseling* (2nd ed.). New York: Lexington.

Visher, E. B., and Visher, J. S. 1988. *Old loyalties, new ties.* New York: Brunner/Mazel.

Roles

Davidson, C. 1993. *Staying home instead: Alternatives to the two-paycheck family.* New York: Lexington.
Lederer, W. J., and Jackson, D. D. 1990. *The mirages of marriage.* New York: Norton.
Stoltz-Loike, M. 1992. *Dual career couples.* Alexandria, VA: American Counseling Association.

Sex Therapy

Leiblum, S. R., and Rosen, R. C. (Eds). 1989. *Principles and practice of sex therapy.* New York: Guilford.
Weeks, G. R., and Hof, L. 1987. *Integrating sex and marital therapy.* New York: Brunner/Mazel.

Spouse Abuse

Geller, J. A. 1992. *Breaking destructive patterns.* New York: Free Press.

Index

Adaptability, family, 115–16
Administration issues, 9–19
  commitment, 12–13
  contract, 12–13, 15–17, 18
  contraindications to SII, 13–14
  dismantling totems and taboos,
    10–11
  healthy collusion, 10
  healthy questions, 11–12
  initial interview, 9
  technique and style, 14
  therapeutic boundary issues,
    17–18
  time factor, 12
  visual technique, 14–15
  in wrap-up, 99–100
Affairs
  SII questions about, 60
  as wrap-up theme, 101
Affection, SII questions about, 50,
  77
Alienating relationship, 30–33
  description of, 32
  predictable pattern clues,
    32–33
Alliance configuration, 6

Anger
  SII questions about, 59, 91
  as wrap-up theme, 100
Assessment of couple, 9–19
  commitment of couple to each
    other, 12–13
  contract for SII, 12–13, 15–17,
    18
  contraindications to SII, 13–14
  dismantling totems and taboos,
    10–11
  healthy collusion in, 10
  healthy questions in, 11–12
  initial interview, 9
  therapeutic boundary issues in,
    17–18
  therapeutic technique and style,
    14
  time factor in, 12
  visual technique for, 14–15
Attaching-detaching marriage, 27–
  30, 97–98
  description of, 28–29
  predictable pattern clues,
    29–30
Attachment, negative, 114

125

About the Authors

WILLIAM J. HIEBERT, S.T.M., is executive director of the Marriage and Family Counseling Service in Rock Island, Illinois. He also serves as adjunct professor of pastoral counseling at The University of Dubuque Theological Seminary, Dubuque, Iowa. He is a fellow and approved supervisor in The American Association for Marriage and Family Therapy and a member of the American Family Therapy Academy. Professor Hiebert is a co-author with Robert F. Stahmann of *Premarital Counseling: The Professional's Handbook.*

JOSEPH P. GILLESPIE, D. Min., is professor of pastoral care and counseling at Aquinas Institute of Theology in St. Louis, Missouri. He also serves as adjunct professor at the School of Social Services of St. Louis University, at Eden Theological Seminary, and at The Family Therapy Institute, all located in St. Louis, Missouri. He is a clinical member and approved supervisor in The American Association for Marriage and Family Therapy (AAMFT).

ROBERT F. STAHMANN, PH.D., is professor of Family Sciences at Brigham Young University in Provo, Utah. He is a fellow and approved supervisor in the American Association

131

for Marriage and Family Therapy, and a Certified Sex Therapist in the American Association of Sex Educators, Counselors, and Therapists. In addition, he is a member of the American Counseling Association and the National Council on Family Relations. Dr. Stahmann is an author of numerous professional articles and reviews and co-author with William J. Hiebert of *Premarital Counseling: The Professional's Handbook.*

Maria A. Rundman, L.C.S.W.
Diplomate In Clinical Social Work
P.O. Box 1679
Ojai, California 93024